Social Media

Series Editor: Cara Acred

Volume 266

Independence Educational Publishers

First published by Independence Educational Publishers

The Studio, High Green

Great Shelford

Cambridge CB22 5EG

England

© Independence 2014

Copyright

Photocopy licence

British Library Cataloguing in Publication Data

Social media. -- (Issues ; 266)

1. Social media.

I. Series II. Acred, Cara editor.

302.2'31-dc23

ISBN-13: 9781861686855

Printed in Great Britain

MWL Print Group Ltd

Contents

Chapter 1: The rise of social media

What is social media? 1

The brief history of social media 2

Social media usage around the world 5

The psychology of social media 6

Want to keep your personal information private? Monitor your online reputation! 7

Majority (71%) of global Internet users 'share' on social media sites 8

Four in ten (42%) of those in 24 countries say social media is important to them... 8

Narcissism on social media tells us a lot about ourselves 9

Esteem issues determine how people put their best Facebook forward 11

Are you addicted to 'virtual' approval? 12

The number of people entering rehab for social media addiction is skyrocketing 13

Online Internet trolls are psychopaths and sadists, psychologists claim 14

How to handle online and social media 'trolls' 15

Silver surfers forgotten in social media boom 16

Chapter 2: Social media growing up

What do young people actually think about social media? 17

Your child's digital profile 18

Half a million children aged 10–15 afraid to be left out of their social circle... 19

Children's Internet use survey offers warning to parents 20

Parents: lose the social media fear!! 21

Younger children and social networking sites: a blind spot 22

Children and advertising on social media websites 24

It's vital we teach social networking skills in school 25

Chapter 3: Positive uses

Social media – it's not all doom and gloom 27

'Social media improves our understanding of major world events' 28

Listen, understand, act: social media for engagement 30

'Work-bound' people and digital travel 32

Five mobile apps for humanitarian aid workers 34

Has social media revived the charity sector? 35

The 'no make-up selfie' craze seems like narcissism masked as charity 36

Ten years' time: social media and the future of fundraising 37

#BringBackOurGirls: the power of a social media campaign 38

Social media could provide early warning of power outages 39

Key facts 40

Glossary 41

Assignments 42

Index 43

Acknowledgements 44

Introduction

Social Media is Volume 266 in the **ISSUES** series. The aim of the series is to offer current, diverse information about important issues in our world, from a UK perspective.

ABOUT SOCIAL MEDIA

Social media sites enable us to share information about our lives, our interests and our opinions. Blogs, tagging, image-sharing, video uploading... the options are endless. With 71% of global Internet users now 'sharing' via social media, this book explores what we share, with whom and how often. It also considers the potential dangers of social media in contrast with its role in raising awareness of charitable causes and potential uses in the future.

OUR SOURCES

Titles in the **ISSUES** series are designed to function as educational resource books, providing a balanced overview of a specific subject.

The information in our books is comprised of facts, articles and opinions from many different sources, including:

⇨ Newspaper reports and opinion pieces

⇨ Website factsheets

⇨ Magazine and journal articles

⇨ Statistics and surveys

⇨ Government reports

⇨ Literature from special interest groups

A NOTE ON CRITICAL EVALUATION

Because the information reprinted here is from a number of different sources, readers should bear in mind the origin of the text and whether the source is likely to have a particular bias when presenting information (or when conducting their research). It is hoped that, as you read about the many aspects of the issues explored in this book, you will critically evaluate the information presented.

It is important that you decide whether you are being presented with facts or opinions. Does the writer give a biased or unbiased report? If an opinion is being expressed, do you agree with the writer? Is there potential bias to the 'facts' or statistics behind an article?

ASSIGNMENTS

In the back of this book, you will find a selection of assignments designed to help you engage with the articles you have been reading and to explore your own opinions. Some tasks will take longer than others and there is a mixture of design, writing and research-based activities that you can complete alone or in a group.

FURTHER RESEARCH

At the end of each article we have listed its source and a website that you can visit if you would like to conduct your own research. Please remember to critically evaluate any sources that you consult and consider whether the information you are viewing is accurate and unbiased.

Useful weblinks

blogs.ucl.ac.uk/social-networking/

www.theconversation.com

www.cumbria.ac.uk

www.debatingmatters.com

www.igniyte.co.uk

www.ipsosotx.com

www.jisc.ac.uk

www.marketme.co.uk

www.mintel.com

news.psu.edu

www.nspcc.org.uk

www.purplewifi.net

www.socialmediatoday.com

www.sourcerise.org

www.uk-rehab.com

www2.uncp.edu

whatdoyoungpeoplethink.blogspot.co.uk

What is social media?

Social Media and Social Networking are terms that are used to describe a wide range of services and applications that either create or encourage an Internet-connected dialogue. There are also a number of interaction and commenting services that will allow for participation on static website pages. Therefore; any Internet-published materials must be considered to be a Social Medium.

These services are not restricted to web-based delivery and may be primarily accessed using other devices, such as mobile phones.

The most important types of Social Media are listed here with examples. This is not an exhaustive list and, because of the changing nature of the Social Internet, should be considered to include new, related technologies and services, as they emerge.

Social networks

These sites allow users to create profiles, share content, comment and create communities of friends around themselves or a product/brand (Facebook, LinkedIn, Miio, Google+, MySpace).

Imagine... you've got the whole world in that!

Scary isn't it!

Video and photo sharing websites

These sites not only permit you to upload and share multimedia content, but also allow for commenting and feedback on content provided by others (Flickr, YouTube).

Blogs, including corporate blogs and personal blogs

Online journals are often presented with the latest entry appearing at the top of the screen. These are very popular and may also encompass some Content Management Systems that are not necessarily labelled as being a 'blog' (Blogger, WordPress, Posterous, Tumblr).

Blogs hosted by media outlets

These are often represented by 'comments' sections on News and Newspaper websites where public feedback is invited on current news stories (*The Guardian*, BBC News).

Micro-blogging

Micro-blogging platforms allow for short message posting, but include similar characteristics to non-micro blogs. Micro-blog messages will often include URLs to longer pieces of work, images or videos. Micro-blogging can also be seen as part of some of the other Social Media platforms in the form of 'Status Updates' (Twitter, Tumblr, Facebook Status Updates).

Wikis and online collaborations

A wiki is a website or similar online resource which allows users to add and edit content collectively. Wiki content is sometimes referred to as being 'crowdsourced' (Wikipedia, WikiHow, WikiAnswers).

Forums, discussion boards and groups

Forums, discussion boards and groups may stand alone or be part of another service or platform. They are usually directed towards a single subject or a group of related subjects and provide the tools to created extended conversations with multiple participants (Yahoo Groups, Google Groups, Whirlpool, UseNet).

Podcasting and videocasting (vodcasts)

These are audio and video files that are available by subscription (often via an RSS or ATOM syndication feed). The originating platform or service will usually provide mechanisms for feedback and/ or collaborative response (iTunes, AudioBoo, SoundCloud).

Online multiplayer gaming and Virtual World platforms

MMORPG (Massively Multiplayer Online Role-Playing Games) and Virtual World platforms allow for gaming and social interaction within an Internet-hosted virtual environment. Social capabilities consist of a wide range of interactive conversation tools and games such as World of Warcraft and Second Life include many of those tools.

Social bookmarking services (folksonomy)

These are services that allow for the bookmarking and collaborative tagging of online content. Bookmarked pages can also receive comments from individual users (Delicious, StumbleUpon).

Social news aggregation

Services that allow for Social Bookmarking of News stories, but may also include the ability to submit user-generated content and/or to vote positively or negatively for any given submission (Digg, Reddit).

Instant messaging

This may include any form of messaging service that allows for delivery of messages to one or more recipients. These messages may be publicly broadcast or intended as private, but as electronic media, they may be released into a publicly viewable location by any of the participants (SMS, Google Talk, iMessage).

Geo-spatial tagging

Geo-spatial tagging is usually accessed via a mobile device, such as a 'smartphone', and provides the abilities to 'check-in' at a location, add reviews to a located service/organisation, provide location specific data to photographs and videos and to create/participate in GeoCaching games (Foursquare, Google Maps, GeoCaching.com).

Personal websites

Any personal website, whether or not interactive capabilities are provided. With the introduction of 3rd-Party commenting/approval services (such as Google Sidewiki, Google +1, Disqus), any static webpage content can become socially interactive.

Product reviews/online shopping

A review site is a website on which personal comments and reviews can be posted about people, businesses, products or services. Many online stores and auction sites also provide the ability to submit reviews of a product or service (DooYoo, Amazon, eBay).

⇨ The above information is reprinted with kind permission from The University of Cumbria. Please visit www.cumbria.ac.uk for further information.

The brief history of social media

Social media are Internet sites where people interact freely, sharing and discussing information about each other and their lives, using a multimedia mix of personal words, pictures, videos and audio.

At these websites, individuals and groups create and exchange content and engage in person-to-person conversations.

They appear in many forms including blogs and micro-blogs, forums and message boards, social networks, wikis, virtual worlds, social bookmarking, tagging and news, writing communities, digital storytelling and scrapbooking, and data, content, image and video sharing, podcast portals, and collective intelligence.

There are lots of well-known sites such as Facebook, LinkedIn, MySpace, Twitter, YouTube, Flickr, WordPress, Blogger, Typepad, LiveJournal, Wikipedia, Wetpaint, Wikidot, Second Life, Del.icio.us, Digg, Reddit, Lulu and many others.

The dawning

1997

⇨ The web has one million sites.

⇨ Blogging begins.

⇨ SixDegrees.com lets users create profiles and list friends.

⇨ AOL Instant Messenger lets users chat.

⇨ Blackboard is founded as an online course management system for educators and learners.

1998

⇨ Google opens as a major Internet search engine and index.

1999

⇨ Friends Reunited, remembered as the first online social network to achieve prominence, is founded in Great Britain to relocate past school pals.

2000

⇨ 70 million computers are connected to the Internet.

2001

⇨ Wikipedia, the online encyclopedia and world's largest wiki, is started.

⇨ Apple starts selling iPods.

2002

⇨ Friendster, a social networking website, opens to the public in the US and grows to three million users in three months.

⇨ AOL has 34 million members.

2003

⇨ MySpace, another social networking website, is launched as a clone of Friendster.

⇨ Linden Lab opens the virtual world Second Life on the Internet.

⇨ LinkedIn is started as a business-oriented social networking site for professionals.

⇨ Apple introduces the online music service iTunes.

2004

⇨ Facebook is started for students at Harvard College. It is referred to as a college version of Friendster.

⇨ MySpace surpasses Friendster in page views.

⇨ Podcasting begins on the Internet.

⇨ Flickr image-hosting website opens.

⇨ Digg is founded as a social news website where people share stories found across the Internet.

After the dawn

2005

⇨ Bebo, an acronym for Blog Early, Blog Often, is started as another social networking website.

⇨ News Corporation, a global media company founded by Rupert Murdoch, with holdings in film, television, cable, magazines, newspapers and book publishing, purchases MySpace.

⇨ Facebook launches a version for high-school students.

⇨ Friends Reunited, now with 15 million members, is sold to the British television company ITV.

⇨ YouTube begins storing and retrieving videos.

2006

⇨ MySpace is the most popular social networking site in the US.

⇨ Twitter is launched as a social networking and micro-blogging site, enabling members to send and receive 140-character messages called tweets.

⇨ Facebook membership is expanded and opened to anyone over age 13.

⇨ Google has indexed more than 25 billion web pages, 400 million queries per day, 1.3 billion images and more than a billion Usenet messages.

2007

⇨ Microsoft buys a stake in Facebook.

⇨ Facebook initiates Facebook Platform which lets third-party developers create applications (apps) for the site.

⇨ Facebook launches its Beacon advertising system, which exposes user purchasing activity. Beacon sends data from external websites to Facebook so targeted advertisements can be presented. The civic action group MoveOn.org and many others protest it as an invasion of privacy. Beacon is shut down in 2009.

⇨ Apple releases the iPhone multimedia and Internet smartphone.

2008

⇨ Facebook surpasses MySpace in the total number of monthly unique visitors. Meanwhile, Facebook tries unsuccessfully to buy Twitter.

⇨ Bebo is purchased by AOL. Later, AOL would re-sell the relatively-unsuccessful social media site.

2009

⇨ Facebook is ranked as the most-used social network worldwide with more than 200 million users. The site's traffic is twice that of MySpace.

⇨ Citizen journalists everywhere are electrified when Twitter breaks a hard news story about a plane crash in the Hudson River. *The New York Times* later reports a user on a ferry sent a tweet, 'There's a plane in the Hudson. I'm on the ferry going to pick up the people. Crazy.'

⇨ Unfriend is the New Oxford American Dictionary word of the year.

2010

⇨ Facebook's rapid growth moves it above 400 million users, while MySpace users decline to 57 million users, down from a peak of about 75 million.

⇨ To compete with Facebook and Twitter, Google launches Buzz, a social networking site integrated with the company's Gmail. It is reported that in the first week, millions of Gmail users created nine million posts.

⇨ Apple releases the iPad tablet computer with advanced multimedia and Internet capabilities.

⇨ AOL sells the relatively unsuccessful Bebo social media site to Criterion Capital Partners.

2011

⇨ Social media is accessible from virtually anywhere and has become an integral part of our daily lives with more than 550 million people on Facebook, 65 million tweets sent through Twitter each day, and two billion video views every day

on YouTube. LinkedIn has 90 million professional users.

⇨ Social media commerce is on the rise along with mobile social media via smartphones and tablet computers.

⇨ Public sharing of so much personal information via social media sites raises concern over privacy.

⇨ Both MySpace and Bebo are redesigned and updated to compete with the far more successful social networks Facebook and Twitter.

2012

⇨ Ever more people are connecting to the Internet for longer periods of time. Some two billion people around the world use the Internet and social media. People also connect to the Internet via handheld music players, game consoles, Internet-enabled TVs and e-readers.

⇨ Social media has come of age with more people using smartphones and tablets to access social networks. New sites emerge and catch on. The top ten social networks are Facebook, Blogger, Twitter, WordPress, LinkedIn, Pinterest, Google+, Tumblr, MySpace and Wikia.

⇨ More than half of adults 25–34 use social media at the office. Almost a third of young adults 18–24 use social media in the bathroom.

⇨ Advertisers look to social 'likes' to enhance brand visibility.

⇨ Facebook reaches a billion users.

⇨ YouTube has more than 800 million users each month with more than one trillion views per year or around 140 views for every person on Earth.

⇨ Public sharing of so much personal information via social media continues to elevate privacy concerns.

2013

⇨ YouTube tops one billion monthly users with four billion views per day, and launches paid channels to provide content creators with a means of earning revenue.

⇨ Facebook user total climbs to 1.11 billion.

⇨ Twitter has 500 million registered users, with more than 200 million active.

⇨ Yahoo purchases Tumblr blogging-social media network, with 170 million users and 100 million blogs.

⇨ Flickr has 87 million users and stored eight billion photos, while Instagram has 100 million users storing four billion photos.

⇨ LinkedIn has 225 million users, while MySpace has 25 million users.

⇨ Pinterest has 48.7 million users, while WordPress hosts 74 million blogs.

⇨ Dropbox has more than 100 million users with one billion files uploaded daily.

⇨ Google+ has 343 million users.

⇨ Reddit has 69.9 million monthly users, with 4.8 billion monthly page views.

⇨ Privacy concerns continue over public sharing of personal information on social networks.

⇨ An Australian survey finds that 34 per cent of social network users logged on at work, 13 per cent at school, and 18 per cent in the car, while 44 per cent used social networks in bed, seven per cent in the bathroom, and six per cent on the toilet.

⇨ Astronauts aboard the International Space Station regularly tweet live from space to a global audience.

⇨ The above information is reprinted with kind permission from the University of North Carolina at Pembroke. Please visit www2.uncp.edu for further information.

© Dr Anthony Curtis,
Mass Communications Dept,
University of North Carolina
at Pembroke

Social media usage around the world

I know what you're thinking. Another social media blog post.

Bear with me here. There's a reason that they are so prolific in the blogosphere, and that's because social media is one of the most vital aspects of mass communication today. It's one of the most prolific and abundant means of getting across what we want to say to anyone, anywhere.

This is not a flash-in-the-pan process. It's not something that suddenly sprung up. It's been an ongoing trend and it doesn't show any signs of halting in the next few years. Half of all adults in the UK, USA, Russia and Spain use social networking sites. This is almost a 20% climb on last year. One quarter of the world's online population logs onto Facebook every day.

Growth in the Middle East, Africa and the Asia-Pacific region have all shown a marked increase in social media usage, ranging from 24% to 31.8% of total adults in those areas. On a global level, visitors will spend approximately five hours on average using social sites per month.

A growing global audience

Remember, this is simply the average. Many countries will spend far more time using these platforms every month. Argentina, for example, spends 9.8 hours, Russia 9.6 hours. eMarketer have stated that Central and Eastern Europe are fully expected to overtake North America in terms of social audience by 2014.

Furthermore, in less than three years, it's estimated that India's online population will grow from 140 million to a staggering 450 million.

Further east, Indonesia is blazing the trail for social. It is currently the third biggest market when you compare number of tweets. This is ahead of markets where Twitter is a dominant social platform, such as the UK and South America.

Not just Google out there

On a side note, we all know that Google is running the show mostly when it comes to search. With 71% of the market, it's important to notice that it is not omnipresent. For example, China is actually kind of a big deal when it comes to the online search game. Their engine, Baidu, comprises almost 17% of the market. Not a huge number you might think. But consider the estimates that China has an online population of 600 million. That means one in every four people using the Internet is from China.

Yandex, a Russian search engine, is actually ranked fourth in the world, in front of Bing.

June 2012			
Countries	**SNS#1**	**SNS#2**	**SNS#3**
Australia	Facebook	LinkedIn	Twitter
Austria	Facebook	Badoo	Twitter
Belgium	Facebook	Badoo	LinkedIn
Brazil	Facebook	Orkut	Badoo
Canada	Facebook	LinkedIn	Twitter
China	Qzone	Tecent Weibo	Sina Weibo
Denmark	Facebook	LinkedIn	Badoo
Finland	Facebook	LinkedIn	Twitter
France	Facebook	Badoo	Skyrock
Germany	Facebook	Wer-kennt-wen	Xing
India	Facebook	LinkedIn	Orkut
Italy	Facebook	Badoo	Twitter
Japan	Facebook	Twitter	Mixi
Netherlands	Facebook	Hyves	Twitter
Norway	Facebook	LinkedIn	Twitter
Portugal	Facebook	Badoo	Orkut
Russia	Odonklassniki	V Kontakte	Facebook
Spain	Facebook	Tuenti	Badoo
Sweden	Facebook	Twitter	LinkedIn
United Kingdom	Facebook	Twitter	LinkedIn
United States	Facebook	Twitter	LinkedIn

Or Facebook either...

When it comes to social media, we tend to assume that Facebook and Twitter is the be-all-and end-all. Whilst Facebook is certainly the favourite for the majority of countries, Twitter still has a long way to go to beat out the competition.

Amazingly, two of the largest online markets in the world (China, Russia) don't have Facebook as their most used social site. In fact, It doesn't even rank in China's top three platforms. For Russia, it comes in third.

Social media is here. It's getting bigger each year. It's becoming ingrained in the online habits of many countries. There's nowhere left to hide from it.

⇨ The above information is reprinted with kind permission from Purple WiFi Ltd. Please visit www.purplewifi.net for further information.

The psychology of social media

By Lisa Lomas

Social media has had a profound effect on the way people engage with each other. Its power lies in the way it can provide users with a sense of personal connection and community. Psychologists are interested in what effect this has on people's behaviour in real life.

Which is the real you?

Social media can have a positive effect on people's confidence. A positive online interaction can make people feel good! Even though users present their actual identity on Social Network sites, they may not be showing their true personas, beliefs, interests or identity. Research has suggested that there is little comparison between a person's updates and posts, to how they are in real life. Online, people have a tendency to present an exaggeration of their personality and there is more time to make adjustments in online interactions. If this is going to increase well-being and a feeling of belonging, then social media is certainly doing its job!

Wilcox and Stephens are right to point out that it is easy to dislike a person's online persona, yet like the person during real-life social interactions. Amanda Lenhart reports that digital use can be beneficial and that one form of socialising doesn't affect another. Just like in the real world we can adjust online behaviour as we gain experience – of course mistakes are made along the way.

Personality and social media

Does online social behaviour reflect real life? Are posts, pictures and tweets a true reflection of oneself? We can certainly present ourselves in a more fabulous way but, words can be misinterpreted and once it's out there we can't take it back!

Wilcox and Stephens also state that sites such as Facebook can increase self-esteem. People naturally present a socially desirable, positive self-view to others when online. In turn, this gives individuals an increase in self-esteem but a decrease in self-control.

Clearly, individuals can choose the information contained in their posts, and keeping up with an online identity makes a person feel good and increases self-esteem. However, the more comfortable we get, the more likely we are to lose self-control and act impulsively online. Other examples of the negative effects of cyberpsychology look at body image in teenage girls, checking romantic partners, sexting online and anger through the Internet.

Reading other people's posts can make us less self-aware, and we increase our reliance on other people's thoughts and feelings. At the same time 'experiencing' other people's thoughts and feelings can also increase understanding and empathy for others. Individuals who interact with people from a wide range of backgrounds and cultures are reported to have higher empathy for others. Without this interaction it is sometimes difficult to understand other people's behaviours and beliefs. Social media is the most fantastic platform for connecting people together who might not meet in real life.

Gaining success in an online interaction would be particularly useful for anxious people, as online interactions could translate into real-life social interactions. Guillermo Farfan, writing in the Association for Psychological Science Observer, warns us that individuals who are socially anxious do not want more 'evidence' that people don't like them.

Initially it was thought that the Internet would be a safe haven for these types, to overcome the inhibitions of face-to-face contact and feelings of isolation. Unfortunately, these are the people who are less likely to use such sites.

For those of you who are wary of posting on social media sites, as we have seen, it can make you feel good. Come on give it a go!

Selfies, Likes and retweets!

There are so many ways to get positive feedback on social media, are we becoming self-obsessed? A study at Western Illinois University found that people who were more self-absorbed reported more activity on Facebook. Dr Newman says an increase in positive interactions, for some, can increase feelings of importance. By receiving 'Likes', new followers and retweets, individuals can gain a confidence boost that could translate into increased confidence in the real world.

These Likes, follows and retweets have been described as 'little pockets of love' and can give users a buzz. It is little wonder that they could be addictive. Researchers in Germany analysed Facebook users and found that receiving positive Facebook feedback produced a high activity in the 'reward centre' of the brain. The pleasure they gained from this was greater than when given a monetary reward! Dar Meshi explains why: 'As human beings, we evolved to care about our reputation. In today's world, one way we are able to manage our

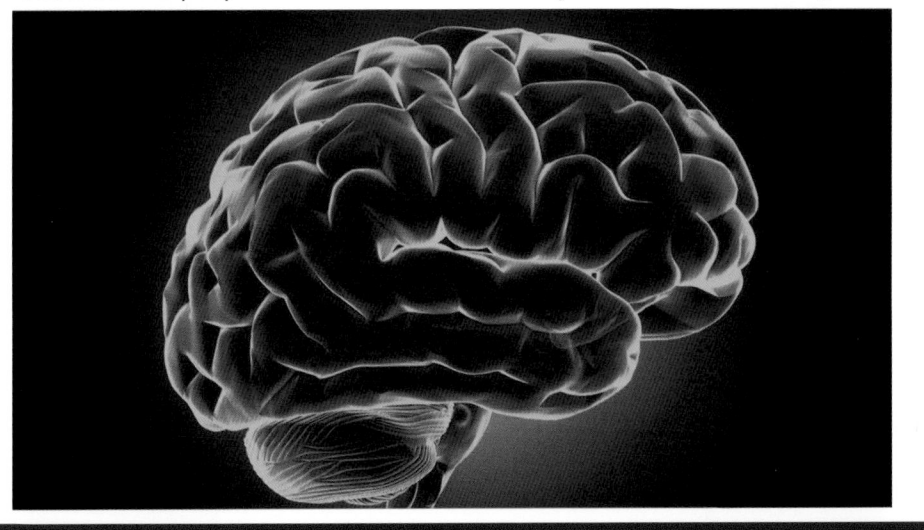

reputation is by using social media websites like Facebook.'

So should we be 'cautious' when using social media?

The psychology of social media is still emerging and in the future we will know more about the effects of life online. Like with any social behaviour we should remain aware of how our behaviour may be perceived by others.

Naturally, we conclude that we know the person we are reading about, and think we know all about their lives from the (filtered) image they project of themselves. Those with a high self-esteem, and a positive filter, are busy posting onto social media sites and this leads to an increase in confidence.

Research by Stoughton, Thompson and Meade investigated whether job applicants' personality characteristics are reflected in social media posts. They found that extroverts are more likely to create posts relating to alcohol, and individuals who are low in agreeableness are more likely to bad mouth others online. Useful for employers and employees alike and a reminder to check our privacy settings!

An interview with a psychologist

Chris Lee summarises psychology and social media:

'Social media is a curated expression of ourselves which we have learned to use in a way that conveys our desired identities.' This feeds our egos and creates our 'Personal Brand' he says. As social media is an extension of personality, then the more reserved are naturally less prone to share content than are the more self-confident users.

He ends with a great piece of advice for anyone using social media, 'behave as if you were with your friends but with your mother in the other room!'

⇨ The above information is reprinted with kind permission from Purple WiFi Ltd. Please visit www.purplewifi.net for further information.

Want to keep your personal information private? Monitor your online reputation!

By Joe Chierotti

Personal privacy is harder than ever to achieve. The abundance of online information, as well as the many venues available to share personal and private information, makes it extremely difficult to protect yourself against online threats to your personal reputation and identity.

Though comprehensive online reputation monitoring may seem impossible, you do, in fact, have tools and methods at your disposal that can protect you from online information predators. There are ways to enjoy the Internet while simultaneously protecting yourself against potential threats to your online reputation and personal identity. Following these useful tips will help you maintain control over your private information and personal identity online.

Tips to protect yourself include:

⇨ **Limiting what you share.** Many people will post intimate and/or revealing details about themselves on a daily basis. The proliferation of social media has made privacy protection more difficult than ever before, which poses the question: what do I NEED to post? Limiting the information you share online provides less opportunity for others to use personal or negative info against you.

⇨ **Be aware of what's out there.** Regular searches of pertinent keywords that relate back to you allow you to, at the very least, maintain awareness of the information that exists about you. Consistent online reputation monitoring can provide you the opportunity to know how much of your personal information is public, and gives you the option to take proactive steps towards either removal or nullification.

⇨ **Use Google Alerts.** Google Alerts is a service that gives users updates as to any new action taken that pertains to a particular and personally-relevant keyword. This allows you to monitor your online reputation more effectively by staying on top of new and potentially harmful activity.

⇨ **Monitor data search sites.** Perform regular checks on data-search sites like Whitepages. com and others to discover what personal information is easily accessible to searchers. Many online information predators scour these sites for personal addresses, phone numbers and e-mails, making it important to know what contact info is easily and readily available.

⇨ **Hire an online reputation management company.** Hiring a professional reputation management company can be extremely beneficial for individuals concerned with keeping their personal information private and protect their reputation online. These companies are equipped with the software and expertise to help you better manage and monitor your online reputation, and are often the best defence against threats to your online privacy.

There are a multitude of ways to construct an effective online reputation management strategy. Monitoring your online reputation requires the employment of advanced tools and proven techniques. When done properly, it will help keep your personal identity and reputation safe from potential threats that exist online.

13 April 2014

⇨ The above information is reprinted with kind permission from Social Media Today. Please visit www. socialmediatoday.com for further information.

Majority (71%) of global Internet users 'share' on social media sites

Seven in ten (71%) online consumers in 24 countries indicate that in the past month, they have shared some type of content on social media sites. The findings reflect a new poll of 18,150 respondents conducted by Ipsos OTX – the global innovation centre for Ipsos, the world's third largest market and opinion research firm. Three in ten (29%) indicate they 'haven't shared any content in the past month'.

The most popular shared item found in the poll is pictures, as four in ten (43%) indicate they have shared pictures online in the past month. Following next are: 'my opinion' (26%), a 'status update of what/how I'm doing' (26%), 'links to articles' (26%), 'something I like or recommend, such as a product, service, movie, book, etc.' (25%), 'news items' (22%), 'links to other websites' (21%), 'reposts from other people's social media posts' (21%), 'status update of what I'm feeling' (19%), 'video clips' (17%), 'plans for future activities, trips, plans' (9%) and 'other types of content' (10%).

Of the online consumers, those from Turkey (93%) are most likely to indicate they have shared any content online in the past month, followed by nine in ten in each of: Mexico (89%), Brazil (88%), India (88%), Indonesia (88%), Argentina (86%), South Africa (86%) and China (85%). This group of highly engaged content-sharers is followed by Russia (79%), Saudi Arabia (78%), Spain (75%), Hungary (83%), South Korea (73%), Italy (71%), Poland (64%) and Sweden (64%) rounding out the middle of the pack. The lower groups of social media sharers begin with Australia (63%), Belgium (62%), the United States (60%), Canada (59%), Great Britain (58%), France (49%), Germany (44%) and Japan (30%).

As for demographics, global averages indicated that those under the age of 35 (81%) are most likely to share any type of content on social media sites, in particular when compared with those aged 35 to 49 (69%) and those 50 to 64 (55%). Women (74%) appear somewhat more likely than men (69%) to have shared some content in the past month. Those with a high level of education (74%) are somewhat more likely than both (70%) low and medium levels of education and income also appears to be an influencing factor: high income (73%), medium income (71%), low income (69%).

17 September 2013

⇨ The above information is reprinted with kind permission from Ipsos OTX. Please visit www.ipsosotx.com for further information.

© Ipsos OTX 2014

Four in ten (42%) of those in 24 countries say social media is important to them: half (50%) of those under the age of 35

Four in ten (42%) of those in 24 countries say social media is important to them while only one quarter (25%) rate it not important. Using a five-point scale, where five means 'very important' and one means 'not at all important', two in ten (18%) rate it with a value of five, two in ten (23%) say four, one third (33%) are neutral at a score of three and 13% say each of two and one.

The findings reflect a new poll of 18,002 online respondents conducted by Ipsos OTX – the global innovation centre for Ipsos, the world's third largest market and opinion research firm.

The big social media story is told in the demographics, especially age. On a global aggregate level, age appears to be the strongest demographic driver of placing importance on social media. Indeed, fully half (50%) of those under the age of 35 rate it a five or four (vs 38% for those aged 35–49 and 30% for those aged 50–64). Women (46%) seem more likely than men (37%) to rate it highly.

The countries with the highest proportions those indicating social media is important to them (score of 5 or 4) are from: Turkey (64%), Brazil (63%), Indonesia (62%), China (61%), India (59%), Saudi Arabia (59%), Mexico (54%) and South Africa (52%). This group of social media lovers is followed by Argentina (45%), Russia (44%), Spain (42%), Poland (37%), Hungary (36%), Sweden (35%), Germany (33%), Great Britain (33%) and the United States (32%). The lower group includes: Australia (30%), Italy (30%), Belgium (29%), Canada (28%), South Korea (28%), Japan (24%) and France (17%).

8 October 2013

⇨ The above information is reprinted with kind permission from Ipsos OTX. Please visit www. ipsosotx.com for further information.

© Ipsos OTX 2014

Narcissism on social media tells us a lot about ourselves

An article from The Conversation.

By Elliot Panek, Visiting Fellow at Drexell University

An increasing number of studies into the correlation between social media and narcissistic tendencies confirm what many of us already suspect. We see teenagers spending hour after hour with their phones looking at Facebook, consumed with how they present themselves online and how others respond to their profiles. We read about self-obsessed celebrities promoting themselves on Twitter, even when they appear to be in the midst of a nervous breakdown. Narcissism on social media runs across the spectrum of users.

But it is interesting how the correlation varies between different sites. In a study we conducted on users of Facebook and Twitter, published in *Computers in Human Behaviour*, we wanted to understand how social media reflected or amplified narcissism. We measured this by asking questions about usage and personality assessments that revealed different narcissistic traits such as exhibitionism, superiority and authority.

We found some young adult university students who had scored higher in certain types of narcissism posted more often on Twitter. But those with narcissistic tendencies in middle-aged adults from the general population tended to post more frequently on Facebook. We concluded that those in middle age had usually already formed their social selves, and used Facebook to gain approval from their peers whereas narcissistic university students used Twitter to broadcast views to broader social circles.

Share and share a 'like'

Studies also suggest a link between the amount of time spent on Facebook and the likelihood of showing narcissistic traits, in particular exhibitionism. However, the frequency with which users post status updates is a better predictor and so a less simplistic measure. We can also begin to dig deeper – if posting frequency is linked to narcissistic traits then it's important to determine whether this applies to any kind of posting (like linking to a news story) or only postings related to one's own thoughts, feelings and accomplishments.

Future research would also determine whether narcissists differ from others in their expectations of how others respond to their posts. For those who receive many comments or 'likes' on a picture or status update, frequent posting can be a means of conversation. If you're a narcissist, how does it affect you if you post but don't receive any feedback?

Research recently carried out at Penn State University also suggests that how we behave in social media reflects our levels of self-esteem. Participants were asked questioned about the types of personal data they included on their profiles, how often they changed and updated information and how they saw their self-worth. From this the researchers suggest that users with lower self-esteem continuously monitor their walls and delete unwanted posts from other users. From a practical perspective, the researchers suggest that app developers could develop ways of customising walls and profile pages to tap into these concerns.

Measure for measure

Social media use has developed over the years. So there is a risk in this type of research of producing fragmentary evidence that doesn't add up to anything meaningful. And the more specific a measure is (measuring Facebook 'pokes', for instance), the more likely the practice that is being measured is to fall out of use, leading research to become inscrutable to future readers (what, exactly, did it mean to 'poke' someone?).

Instead we need to consider the bigger picture by analysing attributes and behaviours that stick around long after the latest iteration of the most popular social media site has vanished. No one may be poking or

tweeting ten years from now, but it's a relatively safe bet that people will post information about themselves and their accomplishments with varying frequency and with various expectations about their audiences.

Moral panic

Some have responded to critiques of social media by likening it to the overblown 'moral panics' over the effect of comic books and television on children. A common defence of social media (and media generally) is that its use is merely an extension of existing behaviour. Teenagers of yesteryear congregated in parking lots; today, they congregate online.

'We need to consider the bigger picture by analysing attributes and behaviours that stick around long after the latest iteration of the most popular social media site has vanished'

This outlook is productive because it helps us to avoid an irrational bias in favour of face-to-face interaction and against all things digital. However, it fails to acknowledge how certain attributes of online life – immediate gratification, the expanded audience – may fundamentally change how we interact and develop as human beings. Keeping an eye on the relationships between social media use and psychological traits such as narcissism helps us know whether certain kinds of online socialising strengthen our social fabric while other kinds divide us further.

More than a billion people now have Facebook accounts and we know that social media use is associated with desirable things such as increasing social support. It also appears to help those who are shy form meaningful relationships. But we have to understand the good and the bad.

'Research findings on narcissism and social media use should help us fill in some of the missing pieces about how we are developing relationships and interacting in a digital age'

Research findings on narcissism and social media use should help us fill in some of the missing pieces about how we are developing relationships and interacting in a digital age. We still don't know whether social media itself causes increases in narcissism, if narcissists merely seek out social media, or if both form a kind of vicious cycle. The rapid, widespread adoption of any technology is oft met with the dual responses of fear and claims of exaggeration. Understanding the limitations of findings – and the benefits – is the best way to separate knowledge from controversy.

24 September 2013

⇨ The above information is reprinted with kind permission from The Conversation. Please visit www.theconversation.com for further information.

© 2010-2014 The Conversation Trust (UK)

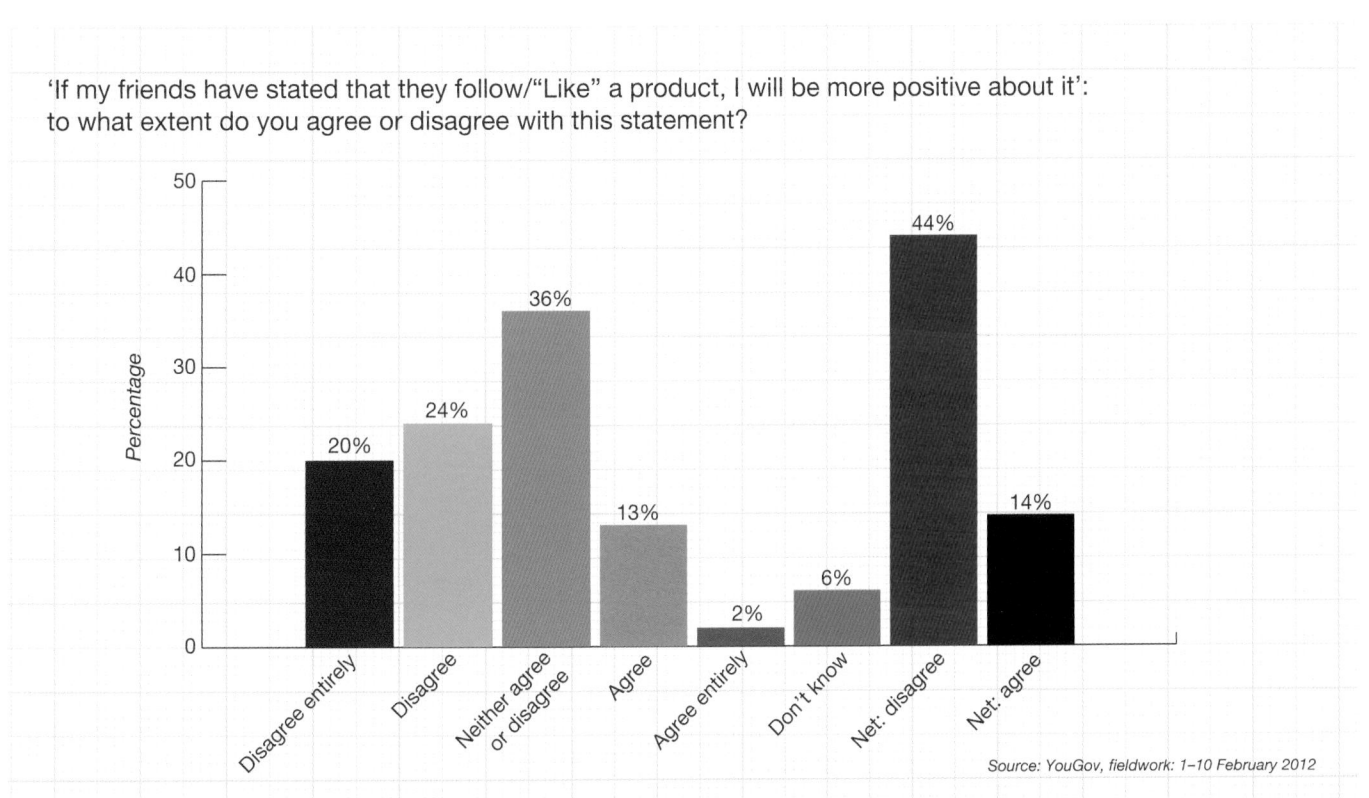

'If my friends have stated that they follow/"Like" a product, I will be more positive about it': to what extent do you agree or disagree with this statement?

Source: YouGov, fieldwork: 1–10 February 2012

Esteem issues determine how people put their best Facebook forward

People with lower self-esteem tend to be much more concerned with what others post about them on Facebook.

By Matthew Swayne

How social media users create and monitor their online personas may hint at their feelings of self-esteem and self-determination, according to an international team of researchers.

'The types of actions users take and the kinds of information they are adding to their Facebook walls and profiles are a reflection of their identities,' said S. Shyam Sundar, Distinguished Professor of Communications and co-director of the Media Effects Research Laboratory, Penn State. 'You are your Facebook, basically, and despite all its socialness, Facebook is a deeply personal medium.'

People with lower self-esteem tend to be much more concerned with what others post about them on Facebook, while users with higher self-esteem spend more effort on adding information to their personal profiles on the social network, said Sundar.

The researchers, who report their findings today (5 September) at INTERACT 2013 in Cape Town, South Africa, said that people with both high and low self-esteem spend time crafting their online personas on Facebook, but choose different paths in that construction. Individuals with higher self-esteem have a greater sense of agency and spend more time adding information about their family, education and work experience to their profiles, according to the researchers.

Users who have lower self-esteem continuously monitor their wall and delete unwanted posts from other users, according to the researchers.

The findings may also lead to alternative ways to make money for online social networks, said Sundar, who worked with Jiaqi Nie, a graduate student in interaction science, Sungkyunkwan University, South Korea.

'The more you get connected to Facebook, the stronger you feel that the items you post – the pictures, for example – are part of your identity and the more likely you are going to view these as your virtual possessions,' said Sundar.

Because both groups of high self-esteem and low self-esteem Facebook users see the social network as an extension of their self-identity, they may be willing to pay for features on social networks, said Sundar. For example, social media and social media app developers may be able to attract paying customers with more customisable walls and profile pages.

The researchers studied how 225 students from a South Korean university filled in their Facebook profiles and how the students edited material that friends linked to or posted on their walls.

Participants answered a series of questions about whether they added information to 33 categories of personal data, including details about their family, work and relationships.

The participants also reported on how frequently they updated and changed information on their walls.

To measure self-esteem and self-monitoring, the researchers asked the participants to answer questions, including ones on self-worth and how they choose to present themselves in public.

The researchers suggest that future studies may investigate how users of different psychological backgrounds take part in other social networking behaviours, such as how often they update photos and how they set privacy settings.

Last updated 23 October 2013

⇨ The above information is reprinted with kind permission from Matthew Swayne at Penn State University. Please visit news.psu.edu for further information.

© *Matthew Swayne 2014*

Are you addicted to 'virtual' approval?

By Kirsty Hanly, Cognitive Hypnotherapist and Coach, Harley Street, London, England

In this age of Facebook, Instagram, Twitter, etc. we are increasingly living our lives through the eyes (and comments) of other people. Have you ever stopped to think about how and what this means to you on a personal, emotional level? If someone 'Likes' your post does that give you a boost? Is your sense of self dependent on how many virtual 'friends' or retweets you have? Are you unconsciously getting validation via these interactions?

Or, do you feel good for just being you?

Don't get me wrong, I love a bit of social media. In my opinion it's a real force for good – particularly for spreading humour, for collecting positive news and as a force for social awareness and change. And for those of us that by all intents and purposes are lone workers (I do technically work with people all day long as a Cognitive Hypnotherapist and Coach, but I'm connecting in a different way!), it's great for connecting up to see how the rest of the world is getting on with things. However, I think we need to look at how we interact with it, what it means for our sense of who we are, and how easily we can all be so much less productive and imaginative whilst engaging in it.

Healthy connections or a time thief?

How could some of that time be better spent learning something new, or reading something inspiring, or finding ways we can really connect with others in a more meaningful way? How could you create more of the conditions for success in your life – both emotional, career, financial?

Often people get caught up in the scattergun approach to living. Doing a bit of this and that but rarely doing those things with full attention. Our IT-busy lives only add to that. Being mindful of where you are at now, with the task you are currently doing can make all the difference.

Are you a Pleaser or a Server?

Super Coach Steve Chandler talks a lot about swapping people pleasing for serving people. I like this idea. Most of us are brought up with an idea that we have to do the right thing. Often our young minds misinterpret this to mean that we have to please the people around us, often at our own expense. This isn't useful to us as human beings. It steals our potential success in life. How much better to serve in a meaningful way – to add value to the world around us. Whether it's by offering someone something that we think might benefit them, or by being the best version of ourselves. Who was it that said 'Be the change you wish to see in the world'? (Ghandi? It's always Ghandi or Buddha, right?) We can all be that change. It doesn't cost us anything except to feel good about ourselves and that can't be a bad thing. This is where social media can be really useful. In spreading ideas or 'memes' in a really positive way. I love that the *Huffington Post* is such a place – where we can interact and listen to each other's often incredibly inspiring viewpoints. The Third Metric space here is one of those places, where ideas and social media can interact for a super force for good.

So the next time you're counting up the comments on your Facebook page, how would it be to have a think about what that actually means to you and how you can balance out your time to develop a true sense of self, either by posting something just for the sake of spreading a good vibe, or by going off and doing something else entirely?

And if you're not sure, you could always create a Facebook survey and see what all your 'friends' think!

31 January 2014

So ... are you the sport car owning executive on Facebook?

The number of people entering rehab for social media addiction is skyrocketing

Engaging in social media is something that most of us enjoy, but some people have become so obsessed with this behaviour that it is ruining their life. There have been a number of reports about this in the media recently – including a report this week in *The Queensland Times* in Australia about how many parents were sending their children to rehab for help. There is plenty of evidence of rising social media addiction in the UK, but nobody is yet stating the obvious – it is becoming an epidemic.

Social media addiction refers to a situation where people are spending an excessive amount of time online – it can also be referred to as Internet addiction. There are probably many of us who spend an unhealthy amount of time on the web, but this is not necessarily a sign that we have an addiction. The real problem is when people reach a situation where they feel uncomfortable when they are not engaging in this behaviour. It has become an obsession and they want to engage in this activity all the time.

Internet addiction is different from addiction to alcohol or drugs because it does not involve physical dependency. This might lead some people to conclude that it cannot be a real addiction. The reality is though, that people can be as dependent on social media as they can be on heroin, and it can destroy their life. It is all about loss of control, which is why Internet addiction is very real.

If you are dealing with social media addiction, there will be a number of symptoms:

⇨ you may have lost interest in other hobbies and now just want to spend all your time online

⇨ you feel uncomfortable about going anywhere unless you have your mobile device with you so you can keep an eye on social media sites like Facebook and Twitter

⇨ other people have expressed concern about the amount of time you spend online

⇨ you have tried to reduce the number of hours you spend online, but you failed to commit to this reduction

⇨ you can't imagine how you would be able to cope without having access to these social media sites

⇨ engaging in social media is getting in the way of your work, social, or family commitments

⇨ you have tried to hide the fact that you spend so much time online

⇨ you may become irritable if other people question you about the amount of time you spend online.

It is important to keep in mind that it is not necessary to have all of these symptoms in order to be dealing with a social media addiction.

In many cases, individuals who are addicted to social media will find it hard to break away from the behaviour without help. This is because there will be underlying issues driving the behaviour and until these are dealt with the individual will continue to act out. Even if the individual does manage to break away from the Internet addiction, they could still turn to other maladaptive behaviours. This is why in many cases the best option is for the person to enter rehab.

Entering an inpatient treatment programme will give the individual the opportunity to get down to the root of their addiction. It will mean that they will be able to look at their real problems and find solutions for these. It means the person will be free and restored to balance.

3 August 2013

⇨ The above information is reprinted with kind permission from Rehab Helper. Please visit www.uk-rehab.com for further information.

© Rehab Helper 2014

Hi Mum, I can't make it to Dad's 50th birthday party today. I just have something really urgent to deal with now.

Online Internet trolls are psychopaths and sadists, psychologists claim

By Kashmira Gander

Canadian researchers have confirmed what most people suspected all along: that Internet trolls are archetypal Machiavellian sadists.

In a survey conducted by the group of psychologists, people who partake in so-called trolling online showed signs of sadism, psychopathy, and were Machiavellian in their manipulation of others and their disregard for morality.

The researchers defined online trolling as 'the practice of behaving in a deceptive, destructive, or disruptive manner in a social setting on the Internet' for no purpose other than their pleasure.

To achieve the results, the team asked Internet users about subjects including how much time they spend online, and whether they comment on websites such as YouTube.

They were also given tests that measured their responses against psychology's 'Dark Tetrad': narcissism, Machiavellianism, psychopathy and a sadistic personality.

Questions also surrounded sadistic statements including: 'I enjoy physically hurting people', 'I enjoy making jokes at the expense of others' and 'I enjoy playing the villain in games and torturing other characters'.

'It was sadism, however, that had the most robust associations with trolling of any of the personality measures,' said psychologists from the University of Manitoba, University of Winnipeg and University of British Columbia in an article published in *Personality and Individual Differences* journal.

It went on to claim that trolls are 'agents of chaos' that exploit 'hot-button issues' to inflame and exploit users' emotions, 'If an unfortunate person falls into their trap, trolling intensifies for further, merciless amusement. This is why novice Internet users are routinely admonished, "Do not feed the trolls!",' the study warned.

The team concluded that those who enjoyed trolling more than other activities, such as debating and making friends, had tendencies in line with the psychological 'Dark Tetrad'.

Perhaps most worryingly, the psychologists based their conclusion on cyber-trolling being an 'Internet manifestation of everyday sadism', rather than merely on online phenomenon.

It is thought the findings may contribute towards a trend of sites such as YouTube and the *Huffington Post* requiring users to comment using registered accounts rather than allowing anonymous posts.

17 February 2014

⇨ The above information is reprinted with kind permission from *The Independent*. Please visit www.independent.co.uk for further information.

How to handle online and social media 'trolls'

By Althea Taylor-Salmon

Whilst we know that social media is an essential part of PR, one disadvantage is that you can't control what negative feedback you might receive. The common name for those who post unnecessarily negative comments on social media are 'trolls'. How you pre-empt and handle trolls should definitely be something you take into consideration when planning out your social media strategy for a campaign. Here are a few things to think about:

Try to avoid trolls from the onset

Making out that your brand is amazing and assuming everyone else will think the same can be a tough lesson to learn. This was highlighted with the Waitrose Twitter campaign 'Finish the sentence: I shop at Waitrose because...... #waitrosereasons'. Waitrose received immense backlash for this (including a few troll comments in the mix!); so remember to be as genuine as possible and not assume anything.

Take yourself through the footsteps of potential trolls

Think about what your comeback might be to your campaign if you were a troll. Go through all possible responses and scenarios and get others involved. Be as honest (and harsh!) as possible. This will help you to uncover any potential negative responses and conversations that could arise and help you be better prepared.

Differentiate troll comments from the genuine ones

Someone might leave you a negative comment but it could be justified and an issue that needs to be addressed politely and professionally from a customer service perspective. If so, it's vital that you are seen to respond to these genuine comments quickly and in a friendly, tactful manner. Trolls, in contrast, will leave comments that are unnecessary, personal, unkind and add no real value to your message. Remember to not take it personally and definitely avoid responding from an emotional mindset. Trolls can typically dedicate much of their time to posting negative comments all over the Internet so you won't be the only ones subject to it. How you handle them will also raise your audience's opinion of you; so use it as a way to rise above!

Have a response policy in place

In most cases, you shouldn't respond at all to troll comments as it's not a productive use of time and trolls like nothing more than when the person or brand they are attacking bite back! However, a few situations might arise where the case should be responded to and managed. Hopefully this possible scenario will have been covered and planned out from the second point above. But if not, take your time to decide the best policy and make your response bespoke so that you don't come across as unprofessional or bitter.

Although dealing with trolls can be a tricky experience, how you are seen to handle them can actually be a great way to add credibility to your brand and campaign. The key is to try and be as prepared as possible.

4 April 2014

⇨ The above information is reprinted with kind permission from Fortune PR. Please visit www.fortunepr.co.uk for further information. The original article can be found at http://www.fortunepr.co.uk/blog/how-to-handle-online-and-social-media-trolls/ and you can follow Althea Taylor-Salmon on Google+.

Silver surfers forgotten in social media boom

An article from The Conversation.

By Chris Norval, PhD student at University of Dundee

Social networking sites such as Facebook and Twitter are an almost ubiquitous part of most young people's lives after just a few years of existence. But the enthusiasm with which they have been adopted by this group has not been mirrored in older generations.

In the UK, Ofcom estimates that 92% of online 16–24-year-olds have created a profile on a social networking site, compared to just 25% of online adults over 65.

This lack of uptake reflects a wider problem. Figures released by Age UK yesterday show that there are just four areas in England in which the percentage of older adults online outnumbers those who are offline. The charity has called on the Government and local authorities to take action to help address the problem that people over a certain age are the least likely to take advantage of online services.

Social networking sites can be a useful platform for communication and interaction and older people have been shown to be particularly keen to use them to share pictures with family.

Research in the past has suggested that intensity of Facebook usage is linked with greater life satisfaction and decreased loneliness. Using these services to connect with children or grandchildren who live far away, for example, can help adults who feel disassociated with family events.

But research shows that older adults have different concerns to the young when they decide whether or not to join up. Because these sites often don't address these concerns, potential older users are excluded from the benefits they offer.

There are a number of potential reasons why fewer adults over 65 use social networking sites. While factors such as not having access to a computer or the Internet do exist, many older adults make a conscious decision not to. This can often be due to concerns over privacy, issues with finding important features or settings on such a site or the fear of receiving abusive messages from other users. Younger people who have spent their formative years getting to grips with technology often take these issues in their stride but many older adults see the risks outweighing the benefits.

While social networking sites designed specifically for people over 55 or 65 do exist, they are often not met with great uptake, and some do little to address the issues and concerns being faced by their target users.

The choice of whether or not to use a social networking site is entirely up to the individual and, of course, there are potentially other complex issues. These include whether a grandchild would want to connect to their grandparents through a medium commonly used as a method for self-expression during teenage years or whether an older adult can really benefit from online communication if none of their friends or acquaintances use it.

Nevertheless, developers can attempt to create the best possible online environment for users if they choose to set up a profile. Sites can be made more inclusive by following age-related development guidelines, using appropriate terminology and running usability studies with potential users.

Working with older adults has thrown up a number of possible options for making social networking sites more inclusive.

These recommendations are currently being researched and the findings will allow developers to avoid many of the common barriers that older adults face. Early usability studies are promising, and findings are due to be published in the near future. Older users could be made more comfortable using these sites if privacy settings are closed-off by default, so their information is not automatically broadcasted. A greater emphasis on reassuring users that suitable security measures are in place is another option, as is making sure that reporting other users is a simple process.

Understanding users is an important step in developing the best possible websites for people. Taking into account these design considerations can reduce the barriers that older adults face, creating a more inclusive website. By investigating how we can improve these sites for older users, we can provide an online environment where a wider range of people can feel comfortable communicating and sharing content with family and friends, if they choose to do so, with implications for life satisfaction and loneliness.

18 September 2013

⇨ The above information is reprinted with kind permission from The Conversation. Please visit www.theconversation.com for further information.

What do young people actually think about social media?

Q: 'How do you think your generation will be defined by other generations to come?'

A: 'Maybe people will say we were more creative, more driven, definitely more competitive... more willing to create different identities just for social media... the creation of fake people, probably not genuine people either'

A: 'Like you can live your life with Facebook, you can be a completely different person, you can be whoever you want to be as long as you are on the Internet and you have got a Twitter account and you know how to say the right things. You have got Facebook and you can make your life look fantastic.'

Today, they are linked inextricably to the phenomenon of social media and attaching a virtual component to their lives is done almost without thought by brands who seek to define them and to engage them. And why wouldn't brands do that? When we spoke to over 1,500 young people this year, 78% of them said they were using social media 'often' or 'all the time'. It makes sense to attach a digital arm to this generation and it makes sense for brands trying to connect with them, to reach them via these media channels.

Or does it?

The thing is, social media has exploded onto the scene and the uptake of social media by people has happened so fast that we're still reeling. Brands have scrambled to climb atop the wave and push out their message via this new platform using a 'tick box' kind of approach. Reach target number of 'Likes' on Facebook? Tick. Adapt core advertising message to 140 character nugget? Tick. Try and 'have a conversation' with consumers online? Tick. Sort of.

The thing is, by using this 'tick box' approach to show that you 'get' social media in the most elementary way, you may be missing the point. Are these ticks actually useful at engaging your target audience beyond surface value recognition? To determine that, you need to unpack why young people are using social media and to understand how they see it fitting into their lives.

Why you ask? Let us tell you

Sure, young people are online a lot and use social media a lot but as everyone knows, this media channel is fundamentally different to the media platforms that came before it in that it is a platform for having a conversation rather than taking in information without comment. Can you imagine if a phone call you were having with a friend was interrupted every five minutes with an advert that mimicked the way you talk to your friend? It's a jarring thought isn't it? It would annoy you, wouldn't it? Accordingly, when brands try to spread their message across this media channel they need to understand the social graces, the cultural codes that dictate appropriate behaviour.

So, we decided to try to expose those codes and to unpack what young people actually think and feel about their social media use. This is where it got interesting.

Our research exposed a sense of ambiguity among young people over the role they feel social media has to play in their lives. They were inclined to be disdainful of over-reliance on social media and of people who showed that over-reliance by sharing too much personal information online.

They did not like addressing the extent to which social media impacted their social lives. Even though most of them are on it all the time and 47% agreed that they use it to stay in touch with friends, only one in five of them agreed 'if you don't use social media, you're missing out on socialising' and 27% strongly disagreed with the statement.

Similarly, while only 18% agreed with the statement 'I use social media to showcase who I am and what I care about', 64% of those surveyed felt that other young people share too much information on social media and 51% felt that other people show a fake version of themselves online. Virtually nobody felt that they were doing it, but over half felt that other people were doing it.

Brands that try to mimic the behaviours young people exhibit online might be missing the mark. Young people might not like being confronted with those behaviours and it might not make sense to them, for a brand to try and occupy their social media space. We know young people use social media, but until we 'get' how they think and feel about this channel, we're shooting blind trying to reach them through it.

An area for exploration, we think...

29 August 2013

⇨ The above information is reprinted with kind permission from What Do Young People Think? Please visit whatdoyoungpeoplethink. blogspot.co.uk for further information.

© What Do Young People Think? 2014

Your child's digital profile

Is your teenager's online presence a turn off for universities and future employers?

Maintaining a positive digital profile is essential for our children who have grown up using the web. But when it comes to helping teenagers find their way in the online world, it can be hard for parents to be sure of the best approach.

How do you keep today's tech-savvy young people safe, while allowing and encouraging them to enjoy the benefits of engaging across social media? What steps can you take to help your teenagers create the online CV and presence employers and admissions tutors are increasingly looking for, rather than lots of tagged drunk pictures and emoticons?

'Today's teenagers are the first generation to have grown up with online in their lives and for them and us as parents, learning how to manage the way they present themselves online is an essential life skill,' says Simon Wadsworth, author of *A Guide to Managing Your Teenager's Personal Information Online.*

'It's about giving teenagers the tools they need to promote themselves sensibly and safely. It's very easy to make mistakes in the online world – and they can have lasting consequences or damage a young person's long-term prospects.'

What's your teenager doing online?

Understand how your teenager is presenting themselves online by following these key steps and carrying out an online 'audit'.

⇨ Search for your teenager's name online, along with their home town, school or club, and see what appears – if any of their social media posts show up in the searches, advise them to change their privacy settings to 'friends only'.

⇨ Assess what different types of devices your teenager has access to; for example, games consoles, computers, laptops, tablets, mobile phones and web cams, and ensure these are securely managed.

⇨ Know which social networking sites your teenager is using, for example Facebook, Twitter, Instagram and online chat and help them optimise privacy and security settings.

Help your teenager understand the online world...

⇨ Explain that their online reputation is determined by what they post online, as well as what their peers post. It is essential they learn how to manage their profiles responsibly.

⇨ Help them to understand their digital footprint – the trail they leave behind every time they use the Internet.

⇨ Explain the consequences of reacting too quickly online and making ill-advised posts.

⇨ The golden rule is that you should only say something online if you would be willing to say it to someone in person.

⇨ Certain topics, for example drugs and alcohol, should be avoided.

⇨ Deleting posts, images and comments after the event may be too late if others have already circulated the content – so think carefully about what you post.

⇨ Make sure they know how to set privacy settings on social media websites such as Facebook and Twitter. They should be set to 'friends only' so that their content has a limited audience.

⇨ Establish basic rules for Internet use and support them to keep their social media profiles clean.

⇨ Advise them never to share 'private' information like phone numbers and addresses publicly and to turn off the GPS 'check-ins' on their mobile devices.

⇨ Monitor how many hours your teenager spends on the Internet each day/week. Place their computer and console in a family area of the home, if it helps to prevent excessive or inappropriate usage. Depending on your child's age, you may want to set up parental controls.

Positive steps – help them create the right impression

⇨ Encourage them to create an online profile that reflects who they are, their interests, hobbies and experiences. Inspire them to set up social media across platforms such as LinkedIn, Twitter and Google+.

⇨ Help them purchase their own domain name, e.g. YourName. com, and to create their own personal blog or website.

⇨ Explain that images they use of themselves online, in any scenario, should be ones that they would want a potential recruiter or admissions officer to see. Advise them to remove unwanted tags on unsuitable posts or images.

Useful links

⇨ http://www.igniyte.co.uk/ online-reputation-management/ wp-content/uploads/2014/04/ A-guide-to-managing-your-teenagers-personal-information-online-FINAL.pdf

⇨ http://www.igniyte.co.uk/ online-reputation-management/ young-peoples-lives-online-infographic/

⇨ The above information is reprinted with kind permission from Igniyte. Please visit www.igniyte.co.uk for further information.

© Igniyte 2014

Half a million children aged 10–15 afraid to be left out of their social circle if not 'always on' Facebook or Twitter

As half term in Britain continues, the sight of teens and tweens constantly connected to social networking sites and devices will be a familiar one to many of the nation's parents. But new research from Mintel highlights the influence of social networking on traditional forms of social engagement for this age group as, today, some 15% of ten-to 15-year-olds in the UK are afraid to be left out of their social circle if they're not always on Facebook or Twitter. This equates to over 500,000, or half a million, children, and the proportion peaks at 21% among 14-year-olds.

Today, 60% of those aged ten to 15 say that they use a social networking website or app – with 39% of those aged ten claiming to do so, 43% of those aged 11 and 54% of those aged 12. This number increases even further for 13-year-olds (73%, 14-year-olds (79%), peaking at 80% of 15-year-olds.

Indeed, highlighting the positive impact that today's young people feel social media brings, some 22% of children aged ten to 15 feel more free to express themselves online, 18% say that their social networking profile or page says a lot about them or describes them best, and 17% claim to spend a lot of time and effort on their social networking profile or page.

And it seems that this age group is also fully equipped with the technology to connect – a quarter (25%) of all ten-year-olds own a smartphone, a figure that rapidly rises with age. Some four in ten (39%) 12-year-olds are smartphone owners, peaking at six in ten (60%) 15-year-olds. Meanwhile some 45% of ten to 15-year-olds use a tablet device in the home, significantly exceeding the 36% overall household tablet penetration in the UK.

Harry Segal, Consumer Research Analyst at Mintel, said:

'Our research highlights the impact that social networks are having on the teens and tweens age group and the pressure they feel to remain connected. There is a burgeoning interdependence between real-life relationships and online interactions among younger generations, and a strong level of demand among children to use social networking sites. In light of this, and the high number of children aged under 13 using them, popular social networks should perhaps focus on providing a safe environment for children, rather than imposing a 13+-only policy that today's tech-savvy tweens find almost trivially easy to circumvent.'

Widespread parental concerns

Today, four in ten (39%) of children aged ten to 15 are friends with their parents on Facebook, and 27% text or call their parents several times a day. However, Mintel's research into teens' and tweens' technology usage also reveals the concerns that parent have on their children's online behaviour.

As many as two thirds (66%) of parents with children aged ten- to 15-years-old are concerned about children interacting with strangers online. This concern is closely followed by fear that their child will be exposed to explicit content online (64%). Worry about cyber bullying online (52%) makes up the top three parental technology concerns. Furthermore, four in ten (42%) of these parents are concerned about children inadvertently spending money online, within a game or within an app, while 38% worry about health risks posed to their child from spending too long using a device. Just 10% of parents are not concerned about any of these issues.

'While explicit content online is nothing new, the rise of social networking likely serves to heighten parental concern over their children engaging with strangers online, particularly as social networks are not commonly blocked by default by parental security software. Whereas previous generations were exposed to 'specialist devices' such as digital cameras, music players and games consoles one at a time – now parents give their child one 'multi-functional' device which gives them personal online access from an early age. So, where desktop computers previously kept children's online interactions in a communal area of the home, the rise of mobile devices means that parents find it more difficult to keep track of what their child is looking at and who their child is engaging with online.' Harry continues.

But while concerns about technology safety ride high, parents are largely willing to grant their children autonomy over their digital activities. More than half (53%) of teens' and tweens' parents trust their children to use their devices without supervision, this declines slightly to those parents of ten-year-olds (41%). In contrast however, today, one in seven (14%) parents admit they simply don't have the time to keep an eye on their children's digital activities, and 13% only let their child use a device when they are in the room. One in ten (10%) always try out a game app before their child uses it.

31 May 2013

⇨ The above information is reprinted with kind permission from Mintel. Please visit www.mintel.com for further information.

© *Mintel* 2014

Children's Internet use survey offers warning to parents

One in five respondents to study of primary pupils claimed to have met someone they had only previously known online.

By Maev Kennedy

Almost one in five primary school age children who responded to a survey on Internet use claimed to have met somebody they had only previously known online. Half of those children said they went alone to meetings in parks, cinemas, fast food restaurants, shopping centres and private addresses. For those who did take somebody with them, half of companions were parents.

A sizeable majority of the children who took the survey were aged between nine and 11 and a significant minority were also regularly awake into the small hours on computers in their bedrooms and were never supervised by their parents.

Almost a fifth said they had never received any training on safe Internet usage – and of those who had, 12% said they found the safety lessons to be useless. Many were claiming to be years older online than their true age.

There may have been some bravado in the answers – 5% claimed they were representing themselves online as aged 26 or over – but it was clear many were able to find their way around the age limits on many sites. A third said their parents had set up their accounts, but 32% were claiming to be 13–15, 10% 16–18, and a further 7% got round the restrictions by using the accounts of older friends or siblings.

Although 18% said they were only allowed to use their social network accounts with parents present, and a further 67% said parents sometimes or regularly looked at what they did online, 15% said their online lives were never checked.

The survey involved 1,162 children in 15 primary schools, all in the south-east or Guernsey. It was started by Tim Wilson, an information security professional and school governor. He was sufficiently concerned at the results from his own school that he extended his survey to other schools where he was introducing the Safe and Secure Online programme, in south-east London, Kent and Guernsey. The results, he said, should be a call to action for parents.

'Bringing the family computer into the living room and having open conversations about potential online dangers will help them play a more active role in the relationships children are increasingly starting online. Parents should ensure their child is comfortable enough to discuss seeing something they shouldn't online. For teachers and schools, the results point to an urgent need for more education on Internet safety to pupils, staff, and parents, especially with Ofsted monitoring pupil attendance and lateness.'

Of the respondents, 7% claimed to have been online after midnight on a school night. As a result, 12% admitted to being late for school and 3% had missed a day.

21 October 2013

⇨ The above information is reprinted with kind permission from *The Guardian*. Please visit www.theguardian.com for further information.

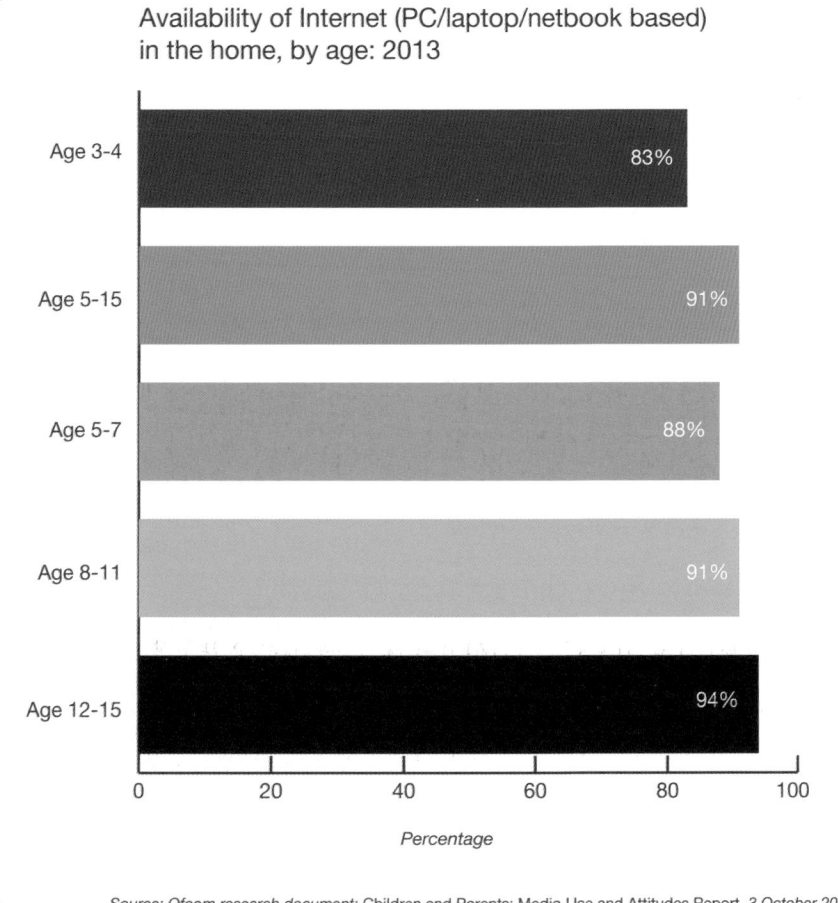

Availability of Internet (PC/laptop/netbook based) in the home, by age: 2013

Age	Percentage
Age 3-4	83%
Age 5-15	91%
Age 5-7	88%
Age 8-11	91%
Age 12-15	94%

Source: Ofcom research document: Children and Parents: Media Use and Attitudes Report, 3 October 2013

Parents: lose the social media fear!!

By Kim Maslin

I often hear parents express fear over their children using social media. This is understandable – there are many things that could go wrong online. But at the same time, there are many things that could go right. I also find that the more parents know about social media, the less the fear consumes them. In order to combat 'social media fear', I propose three steps: education, immersion and communication.

Educate yourself

So often it is the fear of the unknown that is most terrifying.

For instance, I am terrified of swimming in the ocean because I have no idea what monsters may be lurking underneath me, ready to attack. Yet, as soon as I put goggles on…all of a sudden that big hungry Great White is just a tangle of seaweed. The fear is instantly removed as soon as I can see what I am dealing with.

The same can be said for social media. When you do not know what it is, or how it works or what impact it could have on your family – it is scary! And that is amplified when your only exposure to social media is the sensationally spun horror stories so often presented in traditional media.

However, by educating yourself about social media, you can turn it from a lurking shark into a tangle of seaweed. What you will find is that like any other tool, it has both pros and cons, and the outcomes all come down to how you use it.

Communicate with your children

I always like to say, communication is the key. If you have concerns about your children's use of social media – talk to them about it. Now that you have educated yourself on all-things social media, you are in the best position to have an informed discussion with them. Explain to them where your concerns lie and discuss with them the risks and benefits you see social media presenting, and in turn, listen to their opinions and concerns.

Communication is a two-way thing, and odds are your children will still know more about social media than you do, meaning they are also a great source of information. I am sure your children would be more than happy to share some of their social media knowledge with you! In this way, you can engage in social media together, learning from one another and addressing the fear face-on.

Immerse yourself

However, your children, tutorials and even 'experts' like me can only teach you so much!! In order for you to assess the true potential or impact social media could have on your family, you need to understand what you are dealing with. You need to face your fear by jumping right in there and immersing yourself in all-things social media! Create a Facebook account, start pinning on Pinterest and indulge with some viral videos on YouTube. In doing so, you will begin to learn firsthand the power and potential of social media. Hopefully as a result, the fear will continue to fade away… Just like those people who overcome their fear of heights by bungee jumping off a bridge.

8 January 2014

⇨ The above information is reprinted with kind permission from Marketme.TV Ltd. Please visit www. marketme.co.uk for further information.

© Marketme.TV Ltd 2014

Parental agreement: 'I trust my child to use the Internet safely', by age, 2011–2013

Aged 3–4
- 2013: 52 | 32 | 15

Aged 5–15
- 2011: 81 | 8 | 12
- 2012: 84 | 8 | 8
- 2013: 83 | 10 | 7

Aged 5–7
- 2011: 63 | 19 | 18
- 2012: 68 | 19 | 12
- 2013: 72 | 19 | 8

Aged 8–11
- 2011: 82 | 7 | 11
- 2012: 85 | 6 | 9
- 2013: 83 | 9 | 7

Aged 12–15
- 2011: 88 | 3 | 8
- 2012: 90 | 4 | 6
- 2013: 89 | 5 | 6

Source: Ofcom research document: Children and Parents: Media Use and Attitudes Report, 3 October 2013

Younger children and social networking sites: a blind spot

By Claire Lilley and Ruth Ball

Executive summary

'Now, of course, a free and open Internet is vital. But in no other market and with no other industry do we have such an extraordinarily light touch when it comes to protecting our children. Children can't go into the shops or the cinema and buy things meant for adults or have adult experiences; we rightly regulate to protect them. But when it comes to the Internet, in the balance between freedom and responsibility we've neglected our responsibility to children... So we've got to be more active, more aware, more responsible about what happens online. And when I say 'we' I mean we collectively: governments, parents, Internet providers and platforms, educators and charities.'

David Cameron, speech on 24 July 2013[1]

'Many providers ban users under 13 and apply particular technical protection mechanisms and moderated services for minors under 18. However, age restrictions are only partially effective. Fewer younger than older children use social networking sites, but many 'underage' children are still using these services. It seems clear that measures to ensure that under-aged users are rejected or deleted from the service are not successful on the top social networking site services used by children in Europe.'

UKCCIS Evidence Group[2].

Social networking sites are very popular with children and young people and offer users opportunities to socialise, learn, have fun and be creative in new ways through the integration of different functions such as photo sharing, blogging, game playing and instant messaging.

New research from the NSPCC[3] has found that almost a quarter (23 per cent) of 11- and 12-year-olds who have a profile on a social networking site say that they have been upset by something on it over the last year. These experiences range from trolling to online stalking to being asked to send a sexual message. While most of these children were able to recover from what they encountered quickly, around one fifth felt upset or scared for weeks or months after the incident occurred. A fifth of those who experienced something that upset them told us that they experienced this every day or almost every day. Furthermore, the evidence indicates that these upsetting and frightening experiences are not merely an extension of what is happening in the playground. Worryingly, children reported that over half of these experiences were caused by strangers, people they only knew online, or they did not know who caused it.

It is encouraging that 11- and 12-year-olds are more likely than children aged 13 to 16 to turn to parents for help when they are upset by something they see on a social networking site. However, parents are not always certain what advice to give, and some are not

1 Available at: https://www.gov.uk/government/speeches/the-internet-and-pornography-prime-minister-calls-for-action.

2 Livingstone, S., Davidson, J., Bryce, J., Millwood Hargrave, A., Grove-Hills, J. (2012) *Children's Online Activities: Risks and Safety, the UK Evidence Base.* A report prepared for the UK Council for Child Internet Safety by the UKCCIS Evidence Group. Available at: http://www.saferinternet.org.uk/downloads/Research_Highlights/UKCCIS_Report_2012.pdf.

3 The NSPCC surveyed 1,024 children aged 11–16 years old. 28% were aged 11–12 years. Of this group, 23% had a negative experience online.

aware that most popular social networking sites have a minimum age of 13.

Some of the most popular sites, such as Facebook, Twitter and YouTube, require users to be over the age of 13 to have a profile. There is reliable evidence from a variety of sources that large numbers of children under the age of 13 are active users of these sites.[4]

We estimate that around half of all the UK's 11- and 12-year-olds (666,000 children) have a profile on a social networking site for which the minimum age is at least 13.[5] In many cases parents are aware that their child has a profile, and may have helped them to set it up.

Some of the providers of social networking sites with a minimum age of 13 say that they do not provide bespoke advice for children under the age of 13, because they are not supposed to have a profile on their sites. There is a lack of robust age verification tools and children lie about their age in order to obtain profiles. It is very difficult for providers to ascertain which profiles are underage 12-year-old users and which are legitimate 13-year-old users. Other providers are concerned that providing bespoke advice to underage users would put them in breach of the American legal and regulatory framework by which they are governed – a framework primarily designed to protect children under 13 years old from inappropriate advertising. In this respect, the American regulation which is designed to protect

children under 13 is a false friend, and may be doing more harm than good by discouraging sites from providing adequate protection to their younger users. The NSPCC challenges these providers to take a more pragmatic approach to protecting children, and rise to the challenge of the large number of children under the age of 13 who are on their sites. These sites may not be directly targeting younger children, but sites which appeal to teenage users will inevitably attract tweens, who imitate older peers.

Providers should acknowledge their responsibility to these children and their parents, and improve the way they respond to the safety of younger users, for example by working harder to keep them off their sites, setting the privacy settings to the highest level possible, and by providing a range of ways for reporting illegal or offensive content which have been tested with children to ensure they are child-friendly.

Self-regulation has had some impact, but there is a need for UK-based agencies to play a greater role in working with social networking sites to find solutions, and in improving the information available to parents to help them make informed decisions about the risks and benefits of social networking for their children.

⇨ Lilley, C. and Ball, R. (2013) *Younger children and social networking sites: a blind spot*. London: NSPCC. Available at: www.nspcc.uk/blindspot. Reprinted with kind permission.

4 Ofcom (2013) *Children and Parents: Media Use and Attitudes Report*. London: Ofcom; Livingstone, S., Haddon, L., Görzig, A., & Ólafsson, K. (2010). *Risks and safety for children on the Internet: the UK report*. LSE, London: EU Kids Online. Available at: http://eprints.lse.ac.uk/33730/.

5 This figure does not take into account the number of children under 11 years old who have social networking profiles on sites with a minimum age of 13.

Digital footprint survey data from mothers who are on social networking sites and have children under two years old. Source: Digital Birth, 2010.

	Mothers who have uploaded images of child under two	Mothers who have uploaded images of their new-born	Mothers who have uploaded antenatal scans
UK	81%	37%	23%
France	74%	26%	13%
Italy	68%	26%	14%
Germany	71%	30%	15%
Spain	71%	24%	24%
USA	92%	33%	34%
Canada	84%	37%	37%
Australia	84%	41%	26%
New Zealand	91%	41%	30%
Japan	43%	19%	14%
EU5 average	73%	29%	20%
Overall average	**81%**	**33%**	**23%**

Source: Holloway, D., Green, L. and Livingstone, S. (2013). Zero to eight. Young children and their Internet use. *LSE, London: EU Kids Online*.

Children and advertising on social media websites

Advertising Standards Authority Compliance Survey, July 2013.

Foreword by Guy Parker, Chief Executive

Should we be concerned if an 11-year-old girl registers her age on a social media site as 18? Or if a 15-year-old boy pretends to be 25? Does it come as a surprise to anyone that a significant proportion of people under 16 register under false ages online?

Part of our commitment to protecting young people is ensuring we better understand how they use social media. As part of that, we commissioned a survey to find out what ads young people see and engage with online and whether those ads stick to the UK advertising rules.

This article provides a fascinating, and in some respects disconcerting, glimpse into the media consumption habits of children. It reveals that ten participants (42% of all children in our study) falsely registered themselves as aged 18 or over. As a result, they were presented with ads for age-restricted products including for gambling, alcohol, slimming aids and overtly sexual dating services – all categories that are subject to strict rules designed to prevent them from being directly targeted at children and young people.

We place a particular emphasis on making sure ads that children see aren't inappropriate or harmful, so our findings give us pause for thought. What do we do when advertisers are sticking to the rules, but children aren't?

Of course, without downplaying their importance, the findings should be put into context. The fact is that children will see ads for age-restricted products and services in other media. That's why we have rules that govern the content of ads: to make sure that when they are seen by children and young people, they don't appeal to them. Encouragingly, very few of the ads seen by the young people in our survey contained problematic content.

Our report also sits against a backdrop of wider societal concern about how to keep young people safe in an online environment when it comes to harmful sites and adult content. As part of that, the Government has brought together online companies, Internet providers and search engines and tasked them with creating better online filters to help parents reduce the risk of their children accessing potentially harmful material.

There's no escaping that we live in a 24-hour, instant access, media world that has created a host of new innovative advertising techniques and opportunities. A recent report by Ofcom highlighted that almost two-thirds (62%) of 12–15-year-olds now own smartphone devices – up from 41% from 2011. That is significantly higher than the UK average for adults of 50%.

In a world where young people are arguably more media savvy than adults, and with many enjoying unfettered access to the Internet, they're increasingly likely to see material that should be off limits. How then do we as regulators, or indeed advertisers, parents and society, respond? It's not straightforward. Our report shows that advertisers had acted in good faith by taking account of the registered age of social media account holders in their delivery of ads. In light of that, it doesn't seem fair to reprimand them for exposing children to their ads. But this isn't the first report that strongly suggests that a significant proportion of children are registering false details online. We need to reflect carefully on an appropriate response.

So, to start with, we'll be presenting these findings to our council, the body that decides whether or not ads have breached the codes, with a view to exploring whether we need to take a tighter line on age-restricted ads in social media or if further research in this area would be helpful. We're also drawing them to the attention of the code writing body, the Committee of Advertising Practice (CAP), and asking whether new guidance for advertisers on targeting ads online is needed.

While we won't shy away from the regulatory challenges this report raises, there are clearly questions here for advertisers, agencies and social media owners. Collectively, they need to address whether enough is being done to prevent children, by virtue of registering false details, from having access to age-restricted content on social media sites. They need to ask themselves whether they really are doing all they reasonably can not to target children with ads for age-restricted products or services when they know that a significant chunk of the child population is exposed to those ads.

Finally, it's not just about what regulators and industry can do. As a society, we all need to consider whether we could or should be doing more to help set the boundaries in which our children will naturally explore the world around them. Parents are used to setting those boundaries in the real world, but for whatever reason, many feel unable to do so in the online world. There's clearly a conversation to be had.

⇨ The above information is reprinted with kind permission from the Advertising Standards Authority. Please visit www.asa.org.uk for further information.

© Advertising Standards Authority 2014

normal Cairo,' he writes, 'while reading a Twitter feed describing apocalyptic clashes and mayhem' [Ref: Foreign Policy]. Worst of all, the potential speed in which social media can report world events gives a dangerous competition to mainstream media outlets, creating an incentive for journalistic standards to slip, as they did with numerous false reports of Nelson Mandela's death [Ref: International Business Times].

A deeper understanding?

Some suggest that social media has the capacity to improve our understanding of world events by raising awareness of events and stories that other mainstream outlets have ignored. A well-known example of this was the Kony 2012 video, which attempted to focus public attention on the use of child soldiers by Uganda's Joseph Kony in his paramilitary group, the Lord's Resistance Army. Some have sought to praise this style of campaigning journalism: 'The millions who watched the Kony 2012 video and donated or contacted a legislator acting individually and however naïvely, might collectively force some big decisions' [Ref: New York Times]. However, the backlash against the Kony campaign by mainstream media outlets, and its subsequent demise, raise important questions about the dangers of the partial take on events promoted by such campaigns. Arguably the shift away from reliable media outlets to social media, especially blogs, jeopardises our access to reliable facts. Traditional media outlets can fund in-depth reporting and research. They 'can underwrite projects that can take months or years to reach fruition. They can employ editors and proofreaders and other unsung protectors of quality work' [Ref: Rough Type]. None of this is possible with a simple blog, and their lack of accountability frequently leads to neglect of basic journalistic standards like verification of sources [Ref: WordPress]. It is also questionable whether a medium in which acts of trolling fellow users, public figures and celebrities is consistent with producing accurate, reliable information. As one academic puts it, 'the anonymity and dynamic, playful quality of the [Internet] has a powerful disinhibiting effect on behaviour and therefore it may not be one conducive to developing a considered understanding of any unfolding events [Ref: Independent]. Others warn of a stifling conformity on Twitter which drowns out discussion on certain issues once the 'collective spite and collective bile, of a Twittermob is unleashed [Ref: Telegraph].

August 2013

⇨ The above information is reprinted with kind permission from Debating Matters. Please visit www.debatingmatters.com for further information and full references.

⇨ This essay a reprinted from a Debating Matters Topic Guide. Debating Matters is a national competition for sixth form pupils run by the Institute of Ideas. It favours substance over style, encourages in-depth research and robust argument of contemporary controversies amongst teenagers. There are over 100 Debating Matters Topics Guides in the archive to download for free: http://www.debatingmatters.com/topicguides

Listen, understand, act: social media for engagement

By Lis Parcell, senior e-learning advisor with Jisc RSC Wales

Not long ago, social media was a phenomenon viewed by many in education with some suspicion: useful, perhaps, for marketing departments to issue press releases, but surely not a serious tool for academic or professional purposes? After all, isn't Twitter just celebrity chit-chat? What could Facebook possibly have to do with a quality learning experience? Where does LinkedIn fit into the picture?

At first, some institutions were keen to block social media as – at best – a disruptive influence or – at worst – a safety threat. Its path to acceptance as a legitimate communication channel has not been smooth.

Changing behaviours

Yet attitudes and habits appear to be changing. Last year, for example, *Jisc Inform* reported on successful experiences with Twitter and Facebook in a range of organisations, highlighting for example how negative feedback can be turned to positive effect. Examples of social media use are discussed in academic forums such as *The Guardian* Higher Education Network. Meanwhile, in Scotland, a recent analysis showed further education colleges beginning to take a strategic view of social media.

Helped by the increase in availability of mobile devices and Wi-Fi, staff and learners are beginning to exploit social media tools to support learning and teaching, whether as part of assignments or group activities, or to support the creation of more informal personal learning networks.

Social media has the potential to extend beyond learning and teaching to support student engagement in the broadest sense.

The role of social media has the potential to extend beyond learning and teaching to support student engagement in the broadest sense. It offers a new way to develop relationships between the student or learner and their institution, as well as an alternative means to raise awareness of an institution's engagement efforts.

Growing focus on student engagement

Student engagement is clearly high on university agendas but what's driving this?

On one level the uncertain funding environment has focused minds on improving communications and involving learners. At the same time, in higher education, we see a growing emphasis on the student as an active partner in governance, curriculum design, quality enhancement and even in leading organisational change.

A newly-published *Student Engagement Handbook* devotes a whole chapter to students as 'digital change agents', also referred to as digital pioneers. Meanwhile, in the further and adult education sectors, interest in 'learner voice' or 'learner involvement' has not gone away.

The importance of belonging

Because social media is all about participation and relationships, it has the potential to support engagement in the widest sense by:

⇨ Encouraging a feeling of belonging throughout the student lifecycle.

⇨ Helping to create trusted relationships in an increasingly digital, distributed study environment.

⇨ Involving learners/students as partners in their study experience.

⇨ Raising awareness of the student engagement or learner involvement work of your organisation.

Partners or customers?

Any discussion about the use of social media for student engagement has to contend with some important debates. Much of the available advice on social media for engagement has grown out of customer engagement in the global business world and may not transfer seamlessly to UK education.

A tension may be felt between the idea of 'students as partners' and the role of fee-paying 'customers'. Issues can also arise when student engagement and learner voice are simply equated with 'satisfaction', prompting fears that by seeking to engage students through social media we will fail to stretch and challenge them.

To address such concerns, effective social media engagement needs to develop within wider quality and communications processes.

Top tips

In 2013, to meet demand from the higher education sector, my colleagues at Jisc RSC Wales and I produced *Social media for student engagement: 20 good practice suggestions for higher education in Wales*, published bilingually in association with Wise Wales. The guidance has been well received by staff and agencies and we've had some great feedback.

Dr Cliona O'Neill, senior learning and teaching manager, Higher Education Funding Council for Wales, said:

'We welcome the Jisc guidance on social media for student engagement, as this is an area of increasing prominence, and changes the way students engage, and expect to engage, with their institutions.'

The launch was accompanied by a webinar to share a selection of 'top tips' which could be used in any UK post-16 sector. Key recommendations include:

⇨ Listen, don't bark! Today, social media engagement is not self-promotion, it's about listening to your communities and engaging in a conversation with them.

⇨ Think about social media as relationship-building, not only for learners/students but for employers, policymakers, research partners, clients – whoever you see as 'your people'.

⇨ Learners congregate in diverse online and physical spaces: be prepared to meet them where they are,

on their chosen devices and channels – prepare to be inclusive.

⇨ Take a strategic approach in line with your organisation's vision, linking social media strategy to other key processes.

⇨ Ensure all members of the organisation are able to develop the skills needed to succeed in a social media environment – see the Jisc guide on developing students' digital literacy.

⇨ Article originally published in *Jisc Inform*. Jisc offers digital services and solutions for UK education and research. The charity does this to achieve its vision for the UK to be the most digitally advanced education and research nation in the world Working together across the higher education, further education and skills sectors, Jisc provides trusted advice and support, reduces sector costs across shared network, digital content, IT services and procurement negotiations, ensuring the sector stays ahead of the game with research and development for the future.

⇨ Find out more at www.jisc.ac.uk.

Social media landscape

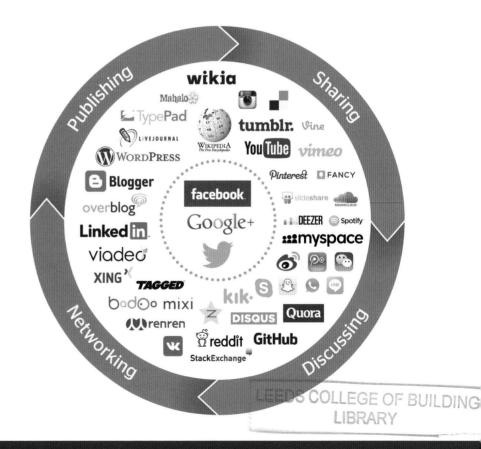

'Work-bound' people and digital travel

By Xin Yuan Wang

One of the research foci of our project[1] is the usage of social media among disabled, house-bound people. As the profile of Dr Karamath in *Tales from Facebook* (Miller 2011), and the story of Amanda Baggs in *Digital Anthropology* (Ginsburg 2013) suggest, social media, or Internet in a broader context, allow disabled people a 'bigger' life. For example, allowing people to express themselves better, to communicate with friends more conveniently, and even gain a 'second life'. Even though I have encountered people who have disabled relatives in their rural hometowns and heard people talking about disability caused by factory work, so far in my field site I have only met one person who has a slight problem in his left leg. I found that it is difficult to find similar examples of appropriation of digital technology among disabled persons at my field site given that most residents live here for the purpose of working.

However, from time to time I witnessed another kind of 'bound' situation which is not caused by physical disability among my 'working class' informants. I called it 'work-bound'. WDG, is a local grocery shopkeeper in his early 40s. His shop opens from 6:30am to 10:30pm (16 hours), seven days a week. He cooks in the shop, has three meals in the shop and even sleeps in the shop since otherwise thieves will visit during the night. He and his family (his parents, his wife and two children) virtually live in the shop 365 days per year. Even though the rent for his shop is not very expensive (around £2,000 per year), he still can't afford to close the shop for a whole day, so it is open every day of the year. He told me that for four years, he only closed the shop once, since he needed to send his mother to hospital on that day. WDG is not alone; most shopkeepers at my field site see 'closing shop for holiday' as a total waste of time and money. WDG is always busy at his shop. People come to post parcels, top-up mobile phone or game points, and buy food and drinks throughout the day. For the purpose of doing business, three years ago WDG installed a desk computer at his shop. Thus, he spends most of every day sitting in front of his computer. It is curious to note that besides pages for mobile phone and digital game top-up, another 'always open' webpage is Google Earth, where he checks different places in the world from time to time. One day, knowing that I study in

> **'We [...] did a couple of things to kill the rest of our five hours in that city – sitting at KFC, staring at our smartphones, uploading photos to QQ and Wechat, and some even played the Wechat online game "tian tian ku pao" while others slept with their heads resting on the table'**

London, WDG skillfully Googled the London map and asked me to show him where I lived in London. He also asked me to show him around UCL campus, and the British Museum nearby. The whole family crowded in front of the computer screen to see the Google map of London, or to use their words, to 'visit' London. I was just amazed and moved at people's pure joy that came from the virtual tour of London in their 12-square metre shop which they were confined to 365 days per year, 24 hours per day.

Compared with small shopkeepers, factory workers have relatively longer 'off-work' time. People who work in factories have two days holiday per month. However one cannot take two consecutive days, which means

---

1   The Global Social Media Impact Study based at the UCL Department of Anthropology is dedicated to understanding the implications of social networking sites for global humankind and society, and explaining their significance for the future of the social sciences.

that most of them can't afford a holiday longer than one day. This month I was invited to join a group of my factory friends' trip to a nearby sightseeing place. From the field site to that place, high speed train takes four hours for one-way, however ordinary train takes almost nine hours. Nevertheless, the high speed train ticket costs around £20 more than the ordinary one, so my friends decided to take the slow train without thinking twice. Therefore, they will spend almost 18 hours in transit, and less than 12 hours at the sightseeing attraction. On Saturday, they managed to leave a half day earlier to catch the afternoon train. On the train out, they played cards for almost nine hours – everyone was so excited about the card playing, even though when they arrived at midnight, everybody was exhausted. The worst thing was in order to save money, they booked a very cheap guest house in a night club district near the train station, and there were stereos blasting in the district until 4 o'clock in the morning. Even though everybody managed to get up at 7am, no one had enough energy to do any sightseeing for the rest of the day. After cans of RedBull, we managed to finish the main sightseeing place in the morning, but after lunch, none were willing to move any more. Thus, we wisely did a couple of things to kill the rest of our five hours in that city – sitting at KFC, staring at our smartphones, uploading photos to QQ and Wechat, and some even played the Wechat online game 'tian tian ku pao' while others slept with their heads resting on the table. The communication between people at the site was very limited, it seemed that everybody felt too tired to talk with each other. Finally, one remarked, 'I have never felt playing QQ and Wechat was a blessing as much as today!' it was a joke which made people laugh. However the fact that my friends came all the way to a sightseeing place to spend a whole uninterrupted afternoon with their smartphones was not a joke at all. Life moved on after the one-day trip, my friends arrived at 6:30 the next morning and had to go straight to work at 7:30am. I checked all of their social media profiles and found that none of them mentioned how tiring the trip really was. Instead, they used beautiful and delightful words to describe how happy they were and how interesting the place was. I felt like going to the place by merely looking at the warm smiles on the

beautiful photos, failing to realise that the place we went to together was actually the same place they talked about on their social media profiles.

The two 'trips' which both took place in November made me to think about the connection and question what digital media means to people in these two trips? It seemed that on the one hand, digital media allows people to experience the world in a way that will never happen without the technology otherwise; on the other hand, digital media have become such a significant and overwhelming part of people's lives to the degree that people somehow need to reconstruct their offline world through the online world. The digital not only in certain degree freed people from their 'work-bound' offline life, but also significantly powered them to construct a much more interesting image of their offline life via social media. Furthermore, I can't help but wonder what will happen if one day my shopkeeper friend WDG finally has the chance to go and visit London, what he will do during his stay in London? Will he still spend a decent time on Google earth or his QQ profile every day given the 'window' offered by Google earth has long been the only familiar and unfailing way for him to see the world?

References

Ginsburg, Faye 2013 'Disability in the Digital Age', in *Digital Anthropology*. Heather A. Horst & Daniel Miller (ed.) London: Berg.

Miller, Daniel 2011. *Tales from Facebook*. Cambridge: Polity Press.

4 December 2013

⇨ The above information is reprinted with kind permission from UCL. Please visit blogs.ucl.ac.uk/social-networking/ for further information.

Five mobile apps for humanitarian aid workers

In recent years, we've seen many exciting and innovative mobile apps hit the digital marketplace – apps that help connect farmers in India to markets, help medical workers gather health data and treat patients in Malawi, and help people fundraise on the go. But what about the aid workers who often risk their lives just doing their jobs? Any helpful apps to make their jobs a bit easier?

So, I'm sharing five mobile apps specifically created for humanitarian aid workers or… the humanitarian at heart.

Global Emergency Overview

Global Emergency Overview is my favourite among the five. This app is beautifully designed and works to inform humanitarian decision makers by presenting a summary of major humanitarian crises, both recent and protracted. It is designed to provide answers to four questions:

⇨ Which humanitarian crises currently exist?

⇨ What has happened in the last seven days?

⇨ What is the situation in the country affected by a crisis?

⇨ Which countries could be prioritised in terms of humanitarian response?

It's a brilliant app for aid workers and those that just want to keep up with world news and crises.

Available for iOS (Apple's mobile devices) and Android.

Relief Central

The Relief Central app aims to assist relief workers and first responders by sharing updates and news from aid groups working on the same humanitarian crisis. The app also shares disaster assessments and response information.

Available for iOS and Android.

iGDACS

iGDACS provides near real-time information about natural disasters and allows you to send back information in the form of a geo-located image and text. The Global Disaster Alert and Coordination System is intended to tap the abundant information about disasters available from people who actually experience them. Reports of the iGDACS users are used to improve the overall situational picture.

Available only for iOS.

Humanitarian Kiosk

The Humanitarian Kiosk app provides a range of up-to-the-minute humanitarian-related information from emergencies around the world. Once installed, you simply select the kiosks that you are interested in and they will be automatically downloaded and synchronised to your mobile device. Downloading the files enables offline abilities, which is extremely important, as we know that most responders do not have a regular, consistent Internet connection.

Available for iOS only.

Voxer

So while Voxer isn't specifically designed with the aid worker in mind, it is the app I most often use when working abroad. I wrote about this app in my last blog post but it definitely deserves a place on this list.

Voxer is a free walkie-talkie-style phone app that lets you talk to anyone in the world using live text and voice. It also lets you send photos. Voxer really does work just like a walkie-talkie – only better, because it records all your messages for playback later. It's especially great for international organisations and aid workers who can use it to communicate with other programme and headquarters staff. No dialing or adding country codes, just hold down the talk button and talk! Brilliant and super intuitive app. Use it on just about any mobile device.

21 March 2014

⇨ The above information is reprinted with kind permission from SourceRise. Please visit www.sourcerise.org for further information.

Has social media revived the charity sector?

By Catherine Boatwright

I just read with interest that 41% of charity heads expect to see an improvement within their organisation as well as in the sector within the next year, and that compares to just 25% who expect it to worsen. These figures are according to data collected by the National Council for Voluntary Organisations (NVCO).

So who's right or wrong? My guess and own opinion is that it will be the 41% who expect to see the growth and let's look at some reasons why.

'Looking through my Facebook and Twitter, I see just about everyone I know doing something for a good cause'

Social Charity Army

Looking through my Facebook and Twitter, I see just about everyone I know doing something for a good cause. Yes, we've just had the London Marathon but there have been ample of competitions, causes and events that people have been getting involved with.

Who can forget the recent flurry of 'no make-up selfies' for Cancer Research, which dominated the pages of Facebook for weeks. The Facebook share and like buttons in all honesty must have been a godsend for many charities out there, who can now rely on the goodwill of the people on social networks to spread their message and get involved.

Never before has the third sector had so much reach and engagement at its finger tips! We even saw the men jumping on the bandwagon doing their own unique style of 'make-up' selfies, after I guess feeling left out! Men were now posting pictures of themselves covered in make-up pouting so much they were giving Katie Price a run for her money.

Everyone's doing it

Other more adventurous fellas decided to raise awareness for testicular cancer by posing for 'cock in a sock' – yes you've read that right, men would take pictures of themselves completely starkers with only a sock to cover their modesty. Doesn't this show the power of social media at its best, all rallying together for good causes in a spirit of healthy competition?

It doesn't stop there with yearly regulars such as Movember and other events taking place, we all know someone who has or will be getting involved in some sort of activity. Right now for example, people I know are jumping out of planes, walking across hot coals, going on sponsored walks, mingling at coffee mornings, getting involved in huge bike rides from one end of the country to the other, climbing mountains, sponsored silences and without a doubt my favourite, The Race for Life. Where thousands of ladies wear pink and together remember the lives of people that have passed and celebrate the people who have beaten cancer.

Optimism

So back to the survey. The charity forecast is a poll for charity leaders and is run on a quarterly basis by members of the NCVO. Usually the poll gets a response rate of around 850 or so respondents and in fairness is showing what appears to be a good level of optimism and confidence in the charity sector.

What's more, for the fourth time running the poll has shown a net expectation in the sector that conditions will improve. This comes following 18 surveys from previous quarters August 2008 and March 2013 when charities thought their situation would worsen and less money would come their way.

I also remember the early noughties when charities were urged by the Office of Third Sector (now the Office for Civil Society) to try and be more business minded in order to become more sustainable, relying less on just donations but more on generating income from multiple sources.

A lot of the top charities have embraced this and we have seen emergences of many social enterprises over the last few years too.

Summary

So, based on the results from the NCVO poll and the level of involvement from what I see from my friends and friends of friends, social media really has to be a driving force and a massive channel for charities.

Equally, with a more business focused mindset to generate income from multiple avenues will also strive to make charities not only sustainable but able to grow and do more of what they set out to do in the first place.

It would be interesting to see if the 41% are at the forefront of social media and whether the 25% are still yet to embrace it to the full.

⇨ The above information is reprinted with kind permission from Intermedia Marketing Ltd. Please visit www.intermm.com for further information.

The 'no make-up selfie' craze seems like narcissism masked as charity

Why not donate instead? If the trend truly is about raising awareness, everyone should at least include a link to a cancer charity.

By Yomi Adegoke

Recently, many Facebook users will have found their feeds subject to even more selfies than usual (and for most, that's a serious amount of selfies). But these are selfies with a difference. Selfies with a cause. No ordinary selfies. Women in their droves have been uploading fresh-faced snapshots in a bid to raise cancer awareness, and by simply exchanging the run-of-the-mill #nomakeup #nofilter hashtag with a caption much more humanitarian, an ordinary selfie now becomes an ordinary selfie masquerading as a fund-raising attempt.

The reason the 'no make-up selfie' trend consistently gets under abstainers' Dream-Matte-Mousse-soaked-skin isn't because it doesn't mean well. We're sure many participants genuinely believe a warts and all Instagram accompanied with a feeble 'My no make-up selfie for cancer awareness xx' caption, has somehow roused a cousin twice removed to visit the Cancer Research site and donate their savings in entirety. But thinly veiling vanity as philanthropy more than irks. The entire thing smacks of the Beyoncé 'I woke up like this' arrogance social media has seen us become so accustomed to. From superfluous 'no filter' reminders to boasts of being bare faced in a profile pic, the pretence these images are for anything other than an onslaught of 'natural beauty' acclamations, coupled with pats on the back for 'fighting the cause' makes the no make-up selfie mania even harder to stomach.

'You can't help but wince at the fact uploading a picture of what you actually look like is now being deemed "brave", especially when being held up against cancer'

If the craze is truly about the cause, why not ditch the Marie Claire and donate to Marie Curie this month? Or seek sponsorship for shirking the MAC? Why not raise genuine awareness through posting admittedly less-sexy cancer stats and symptoms, as opposed to a slightly blurred picture of your best au naturel benevolent pout? Or how about just simply uploading the snap and not skipping out on donating to a cancer charity afterwards? At the very least a simple link to the site of a cancer charity accompanying the self-aggrandising captions would make the whole farce more tolerable.

Even if Macmillan donations do increase because of a few no-slap snaps and conversation about cancer is fostered, so much more can be done with this fad than tagging a few friends and forgetting all about it all soon after. We must truly ask ourselves – what has an image of someone's unmade-up face done for the fight against cancer, that the thousands of other pictures of their made-up faces haven't? This could have been equivocal to Movember ('Makeup-free March' – wasn't hard, was it?) or Dry January for the non-drinkers, but in its current state it simply doesn't cut it. Much of the flack the NekNomination craze received could have been easily evaded, had nekkers asterisked 'to raise awareness for prostate cancer', but at least they remained true to their reason for partaking; showing off.

'The reason the 'no make-up selfie' trend consistently gets under abstainers' Dream-Matte-Mousse-soaked-skin isn't because it doesn't mean well. But thinly veiling vanity as philanthropy more than irks'

You can't help but wince at the fact uploading a picture of what you actually look like is now being deemed 'brave', especially when being held up against cancer. And on realising the movement was actually initiated by author Laura Lippman, who uploaded a photo of her bare face in solidarity with actress Kim Novak after she was criticised for her looks at the Oscars earlier this month, you can't help but feel as though someone has simply taped 'Cancer Awareness' on a pre-made bandwagon, without any intention to aid the fight. The only 'awareness' it seems to be promoting is self. Despite good intentions it's coming across as smug and self-congratulatory, for doing very little and let's be honest – if you're not donating, what are you doing bar seeking praise for having the cojones to ditch the contour?

http://www.cancerresearchuk.org/support-us/donate

http://www.macmillan.org.uk/Donate/

19 March 2014

⇨ The above information is reprinted with kind permission from *The Independent*. Please visit www.independent.co.uk for further information.

Ten years' time: social media and the future of fundraising

By distinguishing a clear need, clear ask and a clear explanation of how a donation will make a difference charities can raise money through social media in the next ten years.

By Lucy Caldicott, fundraising director at CLIC Sargent

In ten years' time social media will have been around for 30 or so years. Online communities began in the mid-90s and blogging a little later. Accessing sites like Facebook and Myspace in the office was frowned upon in those early days and most IT policies had strict restrictions forbidding what were then deemed non-work-related activities. People tended to hide behind avatars and nicknames on social media rather than being themselves.

Since that time, only a few short years ago, the growth both in usage and functionality has been extraordinary.

Social media is now far more firmly embedded in daily life with people far more likely to post using their real name and personal profile. Today it is individuals rather than brands that are playing a strong role in building influence and many charities actively encourage their staff to engage on Twitter and Facebook as they've realised the potential.

This erosion of boundaries between professional and personal has implications for how teams will be managed and structured, particularly those teams that communicate externally with service users and supporters. Everyone's a spokesperson now, so give them the tools to be a good one!

The fundamental benefit of social media for charities and their brands is the ability to connect directly with supporters and to use this connection to strengthen relationships and build trust. Making connections will continue to be important but charities must learn to listen to supporters and engage actively. Customer reviews on sites like Tripadvisor and Amazon are a big influence on purchasing behaviour. Will charities be brave enough to communicate openly what their supporters are saying about them and will that openness influence donor choice?

Charities will have to find the flexibility and nimbleness to use the tools that are available, get better at sharing video content, more used to trying new things, less worried about failing. Perhaps social media will encourage charities to act as a conduit to share their beneficiaries' opinions and experience rather than speaking on their behalf. Perhaps charities will even help their supporters make direct connections with beneficiaries through the tools available.

Service delivery charities are starting to use technology like Skype and Google Hangouts to deliver service online. I predict that this will grow and will have a transforming effect as charities will be able to reach more people, beyond national borders.

I'm old enough to have worked in marketing pre-web. It took organisations a long time to work out what the Internet was even for and many hesitated to create their own websites, worrying about how to manage the 'extra' traffic. Today the web is probably the first place we think to put our messages and online purchasing is enormous. I think the same will become true of social media. It will be mainstreamed into communications plans and will no longer be an add-on or stand alone.

I hope that charities will learn the lessons that social media has to teach about openness and become more transparent themselves as a result. This is what their supporters expect and transparency will bring deeper loyalty. But will it raise any money?

Social media is a two-way communications channel. It's noisy and it's crowded. The beauty of it for charities is that by using it well they can build trust by doing some of the things mentioned above, increase the noise they make by allowing staff and supporters to engage with their publics as ambassadors of their brand, and inspire more people to support them.

And doing all of those things – combined with the basic ingredients that have always been essential for effective fundraising: clear need, clear ask, clear explanation of how a donation will make a difference, loud thank you – will raise you money.

6 February 2014

⇨ This article originally appeared in *The Guardian*.

⇨ The above information is reprinted with kind permission from CLIC Sargent. Please visit www.clicsargent.org.uk for further information.

© 2014 CLIC Sargent

#BringBackOurGirls: the power of a social media campaign

The #BringBackOurGirls campaign has shown that social media is more than just pictures of meals and cocktails.

By Matt Collins

Three weeks ago, more than 200 Nigerian schoolgirls were kidnapped from their boarding school by armed Islamist militants. The event has become an issue of international importance, with a $300,000 (£177,000) cash reward offered to anyone who can help locate and rescue the girls. But the global response started as little more than the outraged tweets of a handful of Nigerian citizens.

At first, the world took little notice of this horrible kidnapping. Oby Ezekwesili, vice president of the World Bank for Africa, gave a speech in Nigeria demanding the Nigerian Government help to 'bring back our girls'. The call was echoed by tweeters in Nigeria using the #BringBackOurGirls hashtag, which has gone on to be used in over a million tweets worldwide.

'For some, a picture of you with a trending hashtag is more of a social statement about you than the abducted girls, one that says, "Hey, look at me, I care about this popular issue just like everyone else!" Even those whose motives are pure may be kidding themselves...'

The Nigerian Government has listened, offered the reward and accepted international offers of help, with David Cameron and Barack Obama both sending in specialist teams to Nigeria to help.

Social media has played a pivotal role in forcing the issue onto the agenda of our world leaders. Hundreds of thousands of people (including the first lady Michelle Obama) have posted images of themselves holding pieces of paper with the #BringBackOurGirls hashtag written on it on Facebook, Instagram and Twitter.

More than any other, the campaign has shown that social media is more than pictures of meals and cocktails – it's a buzzing conversation hub of the important issues of the day. It's populated not just by friends and family; influencers, journalists and politicians are all there too, poised to respond to the problems that matter most to their audience.

Social campaigns as widespread as #BringBackOurGirls are inevitably picked up and taken to newspapers, constituency offices and ultimately the corridors of Whitehall, where online action becomes real.

Like the no make-up selfie campaign however, there is arguably an egotistical element too. For some, a picture of you with a trending hashtag is more of a social statement about you than the abducted girls, one that says, 'Hey, look at me, I care about this popular issue just like everyone else!' Even those whose motives are pure may be kidding themselves that a militant group capable of kidnapping hundreds of schoolchildren will be moved by a picture of a westerner with a stern expression holding a piece of paper.

And are such campaigns even effective? Just look at #Kony2012, a campaign to bring LRA leader Joseph Kony to the attention of the world – a powerful, global social media movement. A movement which ultimately failed (Kony is still at large).

Selfies and hashtags are unlikely to lead to social change on their own – only real governmental pressure and action can do that. But world governments listen, and act, when enough people speak. Social media is the most shareable, durable and global collection of voices the world has ever seen, one which is increasingly difficult to ignore.

Not every charity with their own priority issues should expect their own social media campaigns to go viral. But that doesn't mean they shouldn't try, at least locally.

Every charity has supporters willing to use a hashtag in their posts, to hold pictures of themselves holding signs with inspiring slogans on them. And they do make a difference.

So work with your supporters on a similarly emotive hashtag to rally round – #BringBackOurGirls is a great example, wording which gives responsibility and concern to everyone. Create a Storify of the tweets and posts. Show it to local journalists, councillors and MPs. Not only will it prove your issue matters to people, it will make them act (as the president and prime minister did) to solve it.

9 May 2014

⇨ The above information is reprinted with kind permission from *The Guardian*. Please visit www.theguardian.com for further information.

Social media could provide early warning of power outages

A patent-pending technology from GE could provide a timely early warning solution for detecting power outages.

By Denis Keseris, patent attorney at Withers & Rogers

With the likelihood of power outages in the UK increasing, new technology from General Electric (GE) could provide an innovative early warning system to detect when parts of the grid are running short of supplies, without requiring major investment in infrastructure.

Uncertainty about the future of Ukraine could potentially pose a significant threat to European energy supplies and individual countries could be singled out for blockades. In 2013, Europe imported a third of its oil and about 40 per cent of its natural gas from Russia, a significant proportion of which passed through Ukraine.

Gazprom has already raised the price of natural gas supplies to Ukraine and such increases could start impacting European supplies before long. In a bid to reduce the UK's reliance on Russian oil and gas supplies, Ed Davey, Energy Secretary, has called for 'long-term improvements to energy security'.

With patents pending in the US and Europe, GE's technology makes use of social media channels to provide advance notification of power outages, and their location. Ingeniously simple in concept, the

technology mines real-time data in the form of social media posts across networks such as Twitter and Facebook, in order to establish exactly when and where the outage or 'utility network event' took place.

The technology could potentially fulfil a long-felt need for utility companies to monitor the services provided to customers, without having to invest significant resources in updating infrastructure to enable smart monitoring.

If an outage occurs currently, it can take a number of hours for the energy provider to locate the issue and then deal with it. This is frustrating for customers and can cause unnecessary delays during which homes are left without vital energy supplies.

A system that is capable of monitoring and analysing social media output, identifying and locating posts that use #poweroutage, #powerout or #noelectric, for example, could significantly speed up response times and help to restore supplies more quickly.

GE's European (EP2709047) and US (US20140081998) patent applications may not get a smooth ride, however. Citing specific prior art documentation, the European Patent Office (EPO) has already indicated that, in their opinion, the application may lack sufficient inventiveness because similar systems have been used to provide early warning of earthquakes.

To succeed in securing patent protection, GE will need to show that the way it is proposing to use social media data is a 'technical' solution to a 'technical' problem. If they manage to do this, they could pave the way for other businesses to protect the way they use social media information.

This technology has the potential to provide a solution to an important problem at a critical time, and GE is expected to put forward its case for patent protection strongly. The company may even choose to take advantage of heightened global concern about the future of energy supplies to request that the US patent application be fast tracked.

27 April 2014

⇨ The above information is reprinted with kind permission from *The Telegraph*. Please visit www.telegraph.co.uk for further information.

Key facts

⇨ Facebook was started in 2004 for students at Harvard College. (page 2)

⇨ Twitter was launched as a social networking and micro-blogging site in 2006. (page 2)

⇨ In 2010 Facebook's rapid growth moved it to above 400 million users, while MySpace users declined to 57 million, down from a peak of about 75 million. (page 3)

⇨ In 2013, YouTube topped one billion monthly users with four billion views per day. Facebook users climbed to a total of 1.11 billion and MySpace dwindled to 25 million. (page 4)

⇨ On a global level, visitors will spend approximately five hours on average using social media sites per month. (page 5)

⇨ In less than three years, it's estimated that India's online population will grow from 140 million to a staggering 450 million. (page 5)

⇨ Two of the largest online markets in the world (China, Russia) don't have Facebook as their most used social site. In fact, It doesn't even rank in China's top three platforms. For Russia, it comes in third. (page 5)

⇨ Seven in ten (71%) online consumers in 24 countries indicate that in the past month, they have shared some type of content on social media sites. (page 8)

⇨ The most popular shared item found in the poll is pictures, as four in ten (43%) indicate they have shared pictures online in the past month. Following next are: 'my opinion' (26%), a 'status update of what/how I'm doing' (26%), 'links to articles' (26%), 'something I like or recommend, such as a product, service, movie, book, etc.' (25%), 'news items' (22%), 'links to other websites' (21%), 'reposts from other people's social media posts' (21%), 'status update of what I'm feeling' (19%), 'video clips' (17%), 'plans for future activities, trips, plans' (9%) and 'other types of content' (10%). (page 8)

⇨ Four in ten (42%) of those in 24 countries say social media is important to them while only one quarter (25%) rate it not important. Using a five-point scale, where five means 'very important' and one means 'not at all important', two in ten (18%) rate it with a value of five, two in ten (23%) say four, one third (33%) are neutral at a score of three and 13% say each of two and one. (page 8)

⇨ In the UK, Ofcom estimates that 92% of online 16–24-year-olds have created a profile on a social networking site, compared to just 25% of online adults over 65. (page 16)

⇨ 60% of those aged ten to 15 say that they use a social networking website or app – with 39% of those aged ten claiming to do so, 43% of those aged 11 and 54% of those aged 12. This number increases even further for 13-year-olds (73%, 14-year-olds (79%), peaking at 80% of 15-year-olds. (page 19)

⇨ 22% of children aged ten to 15 feel more free to express themselves online, 18% say that their social networking profile or page says a lot about them or describes them best, and 17% claim to spend a lot of time and effort on their social networking profile or page. (page 19)

⇨ As many as two thirds (66%) of parents with children aged ten to 15 years old are concerned about children interacting with strangers online. (page 19)

⇨ Almost one in five primary school age children who responded to a survey on Internet use claimed to have met somebody they had only previously known online. (page 20)

⇨ 11- to 12-year-olds are more likely than children aged 13 to 16 to turn to parents for help when they are upset by something they see on a social networking site. (page 22)

⇨ It is estimated that around half of all the UK's 11- and 12-year-olds (666,000 children) have a profile on a social networking site for which the minimum age is at least 13. (page 23)

⇨ 81% of mothers in the UK have uploaded images of their child under two years old to social networking sites. 23% have uploaded antenatal scans and 37% have uploaded images of their new-born. (page 23)

⇨ A recent report by Ofcom highlighted that almost two-thirds (62%) of 12–15-year-olds now own smartphone devices – up from 41% from 2011. That is significantly higher than the UK average for adults of 50%. (page 24)

⇨ 59% of the UK's 11–12-year-olds with Internet access have a profile on a social networking site. 23% of these have experienced something that has upset them. (page 26)

⇨ 41% of charity heads expect to see an improvement within their organisation as well as in the sector within the next year, and that compares to just 25% who expect it to worsen. (page 35)

Avatar/Online persona

An image or character that is your visual representation to the online world.

Blog/Blogging

A blog is an online journal where a writer can share ideas, information, opinions and observations. Entries are added regularly and may feature photos, videos and interactive comments left by readers.

Cyberbullying

Cyberbullying is when technology is used to harass, embarrass or threaten to hurt someone. A lot is done through social networking sites such as Facebook, Twitter and MySpace. Bullying via mobile phones is also a form of cyberbullying. With the use of technology on the rise, there are more and more incidents of cyberbullying.

Digital footprint/online reputation/online presence

The 'trail' a person leaves behind when they interact with the digital environment. The evidence left behind gives clues as to the person's existence, presence and identify. It also refers to what other people may say about you online, not just yourself: sometimes also referred to as your online presence.

Digital native

A person who has grown up surrounded by digital technology, such as mobile phones, computers and the Internet (the current 12- to 18-year-old generation).

Digital travel

Thanks to modern-day technology, you don't even have to leave your living room to experience the wonders of the world. With amazing tools like Google Maps, which offers satellite images and street maps, you can virtually explore a city and visit its sights in the comfort of your own home.

Facebook

A social networking service that allows people to connect with their friends and family. Facebook acts as a platform to share your likes and interests, as well as photos, in order to stay in contact and keep up with others.

Google

An extremely popular search engine which allows a person to search the Internet for information about anything they desire.

Hashtag (#)

The hashtag symbol (#) goes in front or a word or phrase to identify the topic of that message. This is commonly used on social networking sites, such as Twitter. On Twitter, when a hashtag rapidly becomes popular this is referred to as a 'trending topic'.

Instant messaging

This may include any form of messaging service that allows for delivery of messages to one or more recipients. These messages may be publicly broadcast or intended as private, but as electronic media, they may be released into a publicly viewable location by any of the participants (SMS, Google Talk, iMessage).

Internet

A worldwide system of interlinked computers, all communicating with each other via phone lines, satellite links, wireless networks and cable systems.

LinkedIn

This is a business-oriented social network for professionals. This allows a person to engage and network with people within their industry. A person's profile is very much like an online CV.

Massively Multiplayer Online Role-Playing Games (MMORPG)

Massively Multiplayer Online Role-Playing Games and Virtual World platforms allow for gaming and social interaction within an Internet-hosted virtual environment. Social capabilities consist of a wide range of interactive conversation tools. This includes games such as World of Warcraft and Second Life.

Social media

Media which are designed specifically for electronic communication. 'Social networking' websites allow users to interact using instant messaging, share information, photos and videos and ultimately create an online community. Examples include Facebook, LinkedIn and micro-blogging site Twitter.

Social networking sites

A place online where people, usually with similar interests, hobbies or backgrounds, can build social networks and social relations together. Examples include websites such as Facebook, Twitter and MySpace.

Troll/Troller

Troll is Internet slang for someone who intentionally posts something online to provoke a reaction. The idea behind the trolling phenomenon is that it is about humour, mischief and, some argue, freedom of speech; it can be anything from a cheeky remark to a violent threat. However, sometimes these Internet pranks can be taken too far, such as a person who defaces Internet tributes site, causing the victim's family further grief.

Twitter

An online social networking and micro-blogging website. This site allows a user to send and read 'tweets' which consist of up to 140-character text messages.

Assignments

Brainstorming

⇨ In small groups, discuss what you know about social media. Consider the following points:

- What are the different types of social media?

- How many do you use on a daily basis?

- What is a digital footprint?

⇨ In pairs, discuss the signs and symptoms of social media addiction. Feedback to your class.

Research

⇨ Try to spend one whole day without using any form of social media. Before you start, make some notes about whether you think it will be easy or difficult and what your biggest challenges might be. Afterwards, write some notes considering the following points:

- Thinking about the notes you made before you started your day without social media, how did your experience compare? Was it as easy/difficult as you thought it would be?

- What did you do to fill the time you usually spend using social media?

- What did you learn from this experience?

⇨ Do you know what your online presence is? Type your name into a search engine and see what information you can find about yourself. Has this changed the way you view internet privacy/security?

⇨ Design a questionnaire that will evaluate how much people care about the way they are perceived on social media sites such as Facebook. Distribute your questionnaire throughout your class or year-group, then gather your results and write a two-page report that explores your findings. You could include some bar graphs to illustrate the information.

⇨ Do some research to find out about positive, unusual and innovative uses for social media. Write some notes and feedback to your class.

Design

⇨ Read *The brief history of social media* on pages 2–4. Using the points you think are the most important or influential, create your own illustrated timeline.

⇨ Create a brief that outlines the design for a social media website aimed at 'silver surfers' (adults over 65). What features would you include? What would your site be called? Make sure you consider any issues that over-65s might have with social media – reading *Silver surfers forgotten in social media boom* on page 16 might be helpful.

⇨ Choose one of the articles from this book that does not have an illustration attached to it and create your own.

Oral

⇨ Are social networking sites beneficial or can they be harmful? Debate this question as a class.

⇨ In small groups, create a presentation that explains the concept of Internet trolls. Your presentation should be aimed at 11-year-old pupils, and should offer advice on how to deal with trolling.

⇨ In pairs, role play the following situation: one of you should play the part of a concerned parent who is trying to discourage their teenage son/daughter from using social media. You should voice your concerns and talk about the negative aspects of social media use. The other person should take the role of the son/daughter and explain some of the positive uses of social media, while also convincing the parent that they can use social media sites safely and responsibly.

⇨ Choose a charity whose work you believe is important and think about how you could promote their cause via social media. Write some notes about your planned campaign and, if you want to take things further, why not give it a go and see what response you get?

Reading/writing

⇨ Visit a blog that you find interesting and write a one-page review for your school newspaper. What does the blogger choose to write about? What are his or her motives for blogging? Why do you like this blog? Would you recommend it to others?

⇨ Watch *The Social Network* (2010) (12A). How does this film portray the topic of social media?

⇨ Imagine you have been asked to describe social media to someone who has never heard of it before, write a definition that is no more than 200 words long.

⇨ Write a short story that explores the way in which social media might develop in the future.

⇨ Read *Want to keep your personal information private? Monitor your online reputation!* (page 7) and write a blog post discussing the importance of keeping track of your online presence.

⇨ 'Children should be taught social networking skills at school.' Do you agree or disagree with this statement? Write 500 words exploring your answer.

addiction to social media 13

advertising and children 24

age and social media use 16

aid workers, mobile apps for 34

Arab Spring 28

Black Dog Tribe 27

blogs 1

bookmarking services 1–2

BringBackOurGirls campaign 38

campaigning and social media 38

cancer awareness campaigns 35, 36

charity sector, use of social media 35–7

children

and advertising on social media websites 24

Internet usage 20

learning social networking skills 25–6

managing digital profile 18

upsetting experiences 22

use of social media 19, 20, 22–3

democratisation of the media 28

digital profile 7, 18

digital travel for work-bound people 32–3

discussion boards 1

education about social networking 25–6

energy supply shortages warning system 39

Facebook

and narcissism 9

and self-esteem 11

folksonomy 1–2

forums 1

gaming platforms 1

General Electric, power outage warning system 39

geo-spatial tagging 2

Global Emergency Overview app 34

groups 1

higher education, social media and student engagement 30–31

history of social media 2–4

humanitarian aid workers, mobile apps 34

Humanitarian Kiosk app 34

iGDACS app 34

inaccurate reporting 28–9

instant messaging 2

Internet addiction 13

Internet trolls 14, 15

Kony 2012 campaign 29, 38

Massively Multiplayer Online Role-Playing Games (MMORPG) 1

mental health benefits of social media 27

micro-blogging 1

misinformation about news events 28–9

MMORPG (Massively Multiplayer Online Role-Playing Games) 1

mobile apps for humanitarian aid workers 34

mothers uploading images of young children 23

narcissism 9–10

news media, impact of social media 28–9

Nigerian schoolgirls freedom campaign 38

no make-up selfies 35, 36

older people and social media 16

online multiplayer gaming 1

online persona 6

online reputation 7, 18

parents

advice for 20, 21

concerns about children's social media usage 19

uploading images of young children 23

personal websites 2

personality and social media 6

photo sharing websites 1

podcasting 1

positive uses of social media 27–39

power outage warning using social media 39

privacy 7, 18

product reviews 2

psychology of social media 6–7

Relief Central app 34

reputation management 7, 18

safety
  concerns of parents 19
  and personal privacy 7
schools, teaching social networking skills 25–6
self-esteem 6, 12
  and social media behaviour 9–10, 11
sharing content, worldwide statistics 8
social bookmarking services 1–2
social media
  addiction 13
  history 2–4
  positive uses 27–39
  types of 1–2
  worldwide usage 5, 8
social networks 1
social news aggregation 2
student engagement 30–31

teaching social networking skills 25–6
travel, virtual, for work-bound people 32–3
trolls 14, 15
Twitter and narcissism 9

underage use of social networking 22–3
universities, using social media to improve student engagement 30–31

video sharing websites 1
videocasting 1
virtual travel for work-bound people 32–3
Virtual World platforms 1
vodcasts 1
Voxer app 34

wikis 1
work-bound people and digital travel 32–3
world events reported on social media 28–9

young people, opinions on social media 17

Acknowledgements

The publisher is grateful for permission to reproduce the material in this book. While every care has been taken to trace and acknowledge copyright, the publisher tenders its apology for any accidental infringement or where copyright has proved untraceable. The publisher would be pleased to come to a suitable arrangement in any such case with the rightful owner.

Images

Cover and pages iii, 3, 4, 6, 9, 15, 22, 25, 33: iStock; page 30: Alejandro Escamillia; page 39: Vladim Sherbakof.

page 34: Icons made by Flaticon

Illustrations

Don Hatcher: pages 1 & 12. Simon Kneebone: pages 11 & 14. Angelo Madrid: pages 13 & 27.

Additional acknowledgements

Editorial on behalf of Independence Educational Publishers by Cara Acred.

With thanks to the Independence team: Mary Chapman, Sandra Dennis, Christina Hughes, Jackie Staines and Jan Sunderland.

Cara Acred

Cambridge

September 2014